NANCY -
MANY BLE
YOUR JOURNL C/K

AN INNER JOURNEY

LIVING YOUR LIFE PURPOSE

BY
KATHY WILSON, CPC

Warrior Priestess Publishing

An Inner Journey: Living Your Life Purpose

Copyright © 2006 by Kathy Wilson

ISBN 0-9768060-0-7
Library of Congress Control Number: 2005937629

Edited by Val Dumond
Cover design by Bookcovers.com
Back cover photo by Gayle Rieber
Printing by Central Plains Book Manufacturing

Table of Contents

Introduction..v

1 – Your Life Values.................................1

2 - Personal Boundaries.........................27

3 – Discovering Your Life Purpose..................51

4 – Creating Your Plan..........................81

5 – Success..105

6 – Motivation and Manifesting......................129

7 – Your Personal Support System.................169

8 – Your Spiritual Support System.................193

9 – Overcoming Fear............................221

10 – Plugging Your Energy Leaks..................245

11 – Self Care....................................271

12 – Rewards....................................287

Resources..302

Faith

When you walk to the edge of all the light you have
and take that first step into the darkness of the unknown
you must believe one of two things will happen:

there will be something solid for you to stand upon
or, you will be taught how to fly.

Patrick Overton
Rebuilding the Front Porch of America, 1997

An Introduction to Living Your Life Purpose

You were born into this world with a purpose. You have important work to do — work that *only you* can do, in order to be of the greatest good and highest service to others.

This work is your life purpose.

People who are living their life purpose are happy, joyous, energetic, and excited about their life. In fact, they're so excited about their lives they can't wait to get up in the morning and get started on their day. Their work brings them satisfaction that's soul deep. Is this you? If so, you don't need this book. (Of course, you can still buy it for someone you know who isn't yet living *their* life purpose!)

If you're not living your life purpose, you *know* what it's like. You may go through your days feeling bored, stifled, stagnated, anxious, stuck, resentful or just plain gritchy. Maybe you're experiencing a combination of several of these. You wish that your life was different, but don't have a clue how to change it... or even what you'd change it into. One thing is certain: you know your life is not quite as satisfying as it could be because there's something very important missing from it.

The dissatisfaction that you feel, in whatever form, is your Soul nudging you… telling you that it's time to do the important work you agreed to do in order to be of the highest service to others on this planet.

Here's good news: *everyone* can live their life purpose and be excited about their life. And the even better news is that you may be closer to accomplishing this than you think.

Changing your life so you're living your life purpose doesn't always mean there will be catastrophic upheaval in your life. Often it merely means getting clarity about the things that are truly important to you, remembering what you're passionate about, and honoring yourself and your work. You may simply need to enhance some elements that are already in your life and reduce or delete others. Many times a simple tweaking of your life in small increments can make a *huge* change.

When a ship leaves port on its way to a faraway destination, the captain can change the course by as little as one degree to end up in an entirely different location. The same is true with your life. Changing one small thing can make a huge shift in your life and start you on your journey of living your life purpose.

In your search for the greater purpose of your life you have been nudged to pick up this book. You're being directed toward that which will assist you in remembering what that work is and how you can integrate it into your life now. We live in a perfect universe in which there are no accidents, only Divine synchronicity.

The reason you're reading this now is that it's time for you to fulfill your Soul Contract by living your life purpose.

It all began before you were born...

...the creation of this life of yours. There was much preparation to be done to ensure that you would be able to do the work of your life purpose. Every detail needed to be in place in order for you to be of the greatest service to others in the manner you desired.

The Contracts

There were many agreements with others that needed to be formed and contracts that were created. Most of these involved experiences you wished to have with others so you could gain the resulting lessons and greater knowledge — all of which you would use as you implemented your life purpose. You chose whom you would have the experiences with and what you wished to gain from it.

Among the more important contracts you created was the one in which you chose your parents. You chose them for the life experiences they could give you, but more importantly, you chose your parents because the traits you'd inherit from them would be invaluable to you as you live your life purpose. You inherited more than your mother's eyes and your father's hair. You also inherited physical and emotional influences that go back many, many generations. The memories of your ancestors — their strengths, weaknesses, talents, abilities, and passions — all this and more is imprinted on your DNA to assist and influence you during this lifetime.

Of all the numerous contracts you created there was one major contract — your Soul Contract. This is *the* main contract for your life purpose. It's the outline of your life purpose and includes the type of work you wished to do, how you wanted do it, and the contracts you created with those who would help you along your path during this lifetime. As you live your life purpose, you're honoring and fulfilling your Soul Contract — and moving into the next level of evolution for your soul.

Your Birthday

You chose the exact moment of your birth so you could have the additional support of astrological influences. When you emerged into this world, the energy fields around your DNA, which are similar to the energy fields around your physical body, were imprinted with the electro-magnetic influences of our sun, moon, planets and other heavenly bodies. Their influence is in alignment with and supports your other chosen influences, such as your inherited DNA traits.

These astrological effects and influences are major clues to your life purpose.

The scope of astrology is far too broad to be included in this book. However, most bookstores carry a selection of books on astrology. If you're not well versed in the subject, I highly recommend that you have your natal chart done by a reputable astrologer. There are many important clues about your life purpose that can be discovered through the knowledge of how the stars influenced you at birth.

The Transition from There to Here

During your birthing onto this planet, you moved from a higher dimension to the lower vibrational frequency of this, the third dimension.

The process of this transition caused you to disremember your Soul Contract as well as all the other contracts you so carefully created.

Knowing this would happen, those whom you contracted with agreed to connect with you at specific, critical times during your life to guide you toward your chosen life purpose work. These people may be with you long term or may come into your life for no more than a moment in order to fulfill their contract with you. Recognizing them and their message is another of the major clues you've set up to guide yourself toward living your life purpose.

About This Book

An Inner Journey was co-created with the guidance from higher sources of wisdom for the singular purpose of assisting you in finding the clues that will lead you to you remember your life purpose. Once you've uncovered your purpose, *An Inner Journey* will assist you in integrating it into your life, so that you are fulfilling your Soul Contract by fully embracing your life purpose.

This is *your* book. Therefore, you can use it any way you want. It's okay to write all over it. You can make notes wherever the impulse pokes at you. Scribble away to your heart's content. Highlight or underline text that speaks loudly to you. You might want to have a notebook or extra paper handy in case there isn't enough room on the page for you to continue with your creative flow.

The most important thing is that you *do* use this book. Take the words, the wisdom and the exercises out into your world. Try them on to see how you like them and if they work for you. Use that which works and discard that which doesn't.

Although the book is structured so that each chapter builds upon the one before it, you don't have to begin at the beginning and do each one in sequence. You can start any place you like. If you feel pulled toward the chapters on creating support systems, begin there. Or maybe you want to jump right in and discover the clues that lead to your life purpose. Start wherever you feel drawn by curiosity, need, desire, or even resistance (often that which we resist is what we need the most). Where ever you start is the perfect place for you to begin living your life purpose.

Take your first step into *An Inner Journey* and begin to live your Divine life purpose.

And now, your inner journey begins....

Your Life Values

When you prepare for any journey, it's important to pack the right things to bring with you. Your travels will be smoother, easier, and more enjoyable if you take the appropriate items on your trip. You wouldn't want to take polar fleece clothing with you to Hawaii, for instance. Taking the right kinds of clothes, your personal toiletries, and any miscellaneous necessities, such as your passport or camera, can make the difference between a frustrating experience and a delightful adventure.

Likewise, having the proper preparations completed before you set off on the journey of living your life purpose will insure that you'll have an easier time of it — and you'll enjoy the trip more. As with any travel, you'll be taking a bag of necessities with you on this journey of living your life purpose. Included in this bag are some very important and fundamental items — the most important of which is your life values.

What are Life Values?

Your life values define *you*, the true inner you, your core essence. They form the very foundation of your life and are reflected in everything you think, feel, and do. They're the basis and the meaning of your life.

Your life values are major, important clues that you set up for yourself to help you remember your life purpose. They serve as guideposts, pointing the way for you and keeping you on your true path. They serve to guide you throughout your entire life. All of your choices, judgments, and decisions are filtered through them, whether you're aware of this happening or not.

Life values are intangible, which can make them challenging to define, since you can't see them, touch them, or smell them. They aren't something you can have or own. For example, money is not a value, although there are some things that you can acquire with it that are life values, such as fun, security, and freedom.

Life values are not what you do, although they *are* reflected in *how* you do it. For example, someone who has a life value of beauty might build a house that is aesthetically pleasing to them. Someone else who has a life value of security would probably care less about their house being beautiful, but they *would* care that it's strong, durable, and has sturdy locks on all the doors and windows. Both people built a house, but *how* they did it reflected their life values.

Life values aren't morals or principles. If you feel righteous or ethical about what you're doing, it's not a life value — it's a moral. Morals are laws, written or unwritten, stated or implied, putting rules to principles and ethics. If you're following rules, you're following principles and not your core life values. There are no laws or rules in life values. They just are.

Life values aren't something you acquire along the way because of the experiences you've had. Those are beliefs. As you go through life and gather experiences you make judgments about what you've experienced. "This is good" or "that's bad"; "she's right" or "it's wrong." These are beliefs which are acquired from the judgments you've made about the experiences you've had. Beliefs can also be inherited. Not only can you get them from your parents, you can also get them from your teachers, older siblings, friends, and any other people who might influence you.

The bottom line difference between life values and morals, principles, and beliefs is that life values come from inside of you. The rest are outside influences.

If there's a certain value you'd like to have then it's not *your* life value. If you want more of a value in your life, or if you have to put effort into achieving it, then it's not your life value either. It's either somebody else's value or it's a "should", which also belongs to someone else. We'll deal with "shoulds" later. Life values come from the core of your being and they come effortlessly.

If you have to have it in order to be happy, then it's a need — either yours or someone else's. You don't *need* a life value. You already have a complete set of them.

Life values are not difficult. Life values are as much a part of you as the fingers on your hands. You don't have to work for them or follow rules to get them.

You can't wish them away or trade them in on others that you like better. Most people wouldn't trade their life values for any other values anyway. They *love* the life values they have and are darn proud of them.

3

Most people have between ten and fifteen primary life values. While these core life values don't change or go away during their lifetime, they may change places in priority for a time in accordance with life experiences.

There are usually from three to five core life values that are permanently at the top of their list.

Your Life Values and Life Purpose

Your life values have been with you since before you were birthed and will continue to be with you until the end of your days in this lifetime. You chose them as a part of your Soul Contract for this lifetime in order to assist you in living your life purpose. Your life values are *always* in direct alignment with this purpose.

Before you were birthed onto this planet, you chose the life values which would be most important to you and would predominate in your life. These are major clues that you set up for yourself so you could remember your life purpose — guideposts that point you toward your true life path. Your life purpose and your life values mesh like well-oiled gears.

As an example, a person who chose to be of service to others by doing healing work related to teaching may have core life values of knowledge, wisdom, humor, learning, and creativity. They would most likely *not* have life values of romance, recognition, fame, wealth, and power.

How Do Life Values Work?

Remember that *everything* you do or think is filtered through your life values, including...

The people who attract you. They have life values compatible to yours, which serves as reinforcement for you and encourages you to honor your life values. More importantly, these people are the ones who will be your strongest supporters as you're living your life purpose.

The people you dislike or who repulse you. These people have life values incompatible with yours. They mirror for you the downside of what happens when you don't honor your life values. These are the people who will not support you in living your life purpose. However, they have an important position to play, which will be discussed later.

Activities you enjoy. They're in direct alignment with your life values. Those that you dislike — the kind that drain your energy and leave you feeling disgruntled — are directly opposed to your life values. Both of these types of activities — those you like and those you dislike — are major clues about the nature of your life purpose and we'll play with them further along.

Environments. Those that aren't pleasing to you aren't in alignment with your life values. A person whose life values include peace, simplicity, and privacy would be much happier living in the country than in a busy, noisy, heavily populated city. The environment you're most comfortable in offers another clue to your life purpose.

That which is in alignment with your core life values, whether it's another person's behavior, a situation or event, an environment, or an object, will be pleasing to you. You'll find yourself unquestionably attracted to it.

If it's not in alignment with your life values, you'll find yourself uncomfortable with it in some respect. When you're around it you'll have a sensation of being repulsed, which will manifest as some form of negative emotion such as fear, distaste, impatience, anger, or resentment.

These sensations are your soul at work, gently guiding you toward your life purpose.

Your Automatic Filtering System at Work

Everything you do, say, and think is filtered through your life values, whether you're aware of it or not. Every choice you make is either in alignment with your life values or not. Each choice you make that's in alignment with your life values will be beneficial to you somehow and your life will be made better because of it. If the choice you make is contrary to your life values, you'll experience difficulties with the results.

For example, assume that a person has truth as one of their most important life values. Perhaps their definition of it is the same that our court system uses to swear in someone who's going on the stand…"the truth, the whole truth, and nothing but the truth." That definition pretty much covers it all. When that person then omits a part of that definition in their communications with people, they'll suffer the consequences of their choice.

If, for instance, they neglect to tell a potential client that *all* communication, including emails and phone calls, is considered billable hours, they'll face an uncomfortable quandary every time they have a conversation with the client. Do they bill them for their time and expertise even though they didn't make it clear that this would happen? Or do they eat the time and lose the revenue? If they choose to not bill the client, are they going to feel resentful towards them afterwards? And how much time and energy do they want to waste on tossing this issue back and forth before they finally make a decision they can live with?

As you can see, by being truthful with the client to the full definition of their value and telling them clearly that they will be billed for all the time spent in communication with them, their life is *much* easier and smoother.

When you consciously choose to honor your life values, you too will have a life that is easier, more effortless, and flows more smoothly. The choices you face will become easier to make as you get more clear about your life values, and the choices you make will lead you to a higher quality of life. You'll be living your life congruent with your life purpose — the meaningful work you desired to do this lifetime in order to be of service to others.

Getting Control of Your Life

If you choose not to honor your life values, you'll find your life is more difficult. You may feel like you have little or no control over your life, and this is exactly what happens. When you aren't honoring your life values, you're living by default. You're allowing other people to make decisions for you and, by doing so, you put yourself in the position of being a victim. Each time you allow outside influences such as other people, situations, conditions, and anything in your environment to determine your choices, you're giving away your personal power. Without your personal power you lose your direction and focus, which causes you to move away from rather than toward your life purpose.

When you live your life based on your life values, *you* are the one making the choices about your life.

Who else could possibly know what's best for you?

What's that you say? Your mother? I don't want to give mothers a bad rap, but despite that knock-kneed cliché, your mother doesn't always know what's best for you. This is especially true after you've reached adulthood. Neither do your teachers, bosses, co-workers, friends, lovers, or other family members know what's in your best interest. *You* are the only one who knows the choices which are best for you.

If you're having difficulty making an important decision, it's because you aren't clear about your life values. One you've identified your most important life values it becomes easier and simpler to make choices. When you make a choice that isn't in alignment with them, the results will make your life more difficult. It's that simple. You'll have ample opportunity to play with how your life values affect you throughout this book.

Your life values are the brightly-lit neon signs pointing you toward your life purpose. If you're ready to begin living your life purpose, then you're ready to take the first step — identifying your life values.

Identifying *Your* Life Values

Some people know without a trace of doubt what their main life values are. Just ask anyone what's most important to them and in most instances the answer is their number one life value. When I asked my wonderfully wacky "80something" neighbor that question, she didn't hesitate for a New York second before answering "equitability." It's most important to her that things are fair, and that's exactly how she lives.

For the majority of us humans, however, recognizing our life values can be somewhat of a challenge. I'd hazard a guess that about 85% of the general populace has never given a moment's thought to their life values, much less clearly understand what they are. After having read to this point, you're in the elite 15% who at least know what life values are.

On the next page is a sample list of some values. Select ten values that are most important to you and write them in the numbered spaces below the list. You can combine values, such as honesty/ truth or risk/adventure if the combination seems to define them more completely for you. You can also add any values of yours that don't appear in this list.

Before you get into this exercise, here's an important note: For the purpose of this exercise, love is defined as an emotion, not a value. Think of the choices this way: almost every value in this list can be one of the many different faces of love.

To help you, here's a review of guidelines what life values are not:
> **Morals** give you a feeling of being righteous or ethical.
> **Principles** follow rules.
> **"Shoulds"** don't come easily and usually feel forced.
> **Needs** are what you think is necessary for you to have in order to be happy.
> **Beliefs** are acquired from life experiences.
> **Emotions** are what you feel.

Humor	Directness	Honesty	Partnership
Productivity	Service	Contribution	Excellence
Freedom	Focus	Romance	Recognition
Harmony	Orderliness	Success	Accomplishment
Accuracy	Adventure	Zest	Tradition
Fame	Growth	Beauty	Participation
Performance	Collaboration	Community	Connectedness
Friendship	Lightness	Spirituality	Empowerment
Integrity	Creativity	Independence	Self expression
Nurturing	Joy	Authenticity	Acknowledgement
Risk	Peace	Elegance	Safety
Vitality	Trust	Security	Clarity
Wisdom	Curiosity	Leadership	Knowledge
Justice	Leisure	Learning	Kindness
Intelligence	Privacy	Humility	Family
Generosity	Charity	Comfort	Individuality
Honor	Dignity	Intimacy	Simplicity
Power	Strength		

List your top ten life values here:
1.
2.
3.
4.
5.
6.
7.
8.
9.
10.

Having trouble identifying your top ten life values? Here are some helpful hints to make the process easier.

1. Start by deleting those that you know aren't very important to you. Then go through the list again and eliminate those that are questionable — the "maybes." After doing that, you should be getting down to the nitty-gritty in your list.

2. Cross out any that you absolutely *know* aren't your life values; then cross out the ones that you *think* aren't yours. Now cross out any that just don't *seem to be* your values. Go through whatever is left and pick your ten most important values.

3. Enlist the help of some of your friends. Make copies of the list of values and give a copy to a few people who know you, and who you can trust to be honest but *not* brutal or cruel. Have them choose ten values that they see you exhibiting most often.

4. Think of ten people who you admire. What are the qualities about them that you admire? These qualities are values that you're in alignment with and are the same or similar to your life values.

5. Think about some of the most important people that you've chosen to have in your life, such as your best friends. (These are people you choose to have in your life, not people you have little or no choice about, like family or bosses.) What are some of their qualities that you admire? You use these qualities filter when you select whom you want in your life.

What's Important to You?

Still unsure of what your core life values are? Answer the following questions. (There may be more than one value in each answer. That's ok. At the end you'll sort through them.)

What's most important to you about today?

What's most important to you about the work you do?

What's most important to you about your community?

What's most important to you about your home?

What's most important to you about your money and finances?

What's most important to you about your life partner?

Now, go through your answers and see what common themes you find, or what words are repeated or seem to stand out. Add those to your list which you recognize as your life values.

Reflections of Your Life Values

If you're still not clear about what your life values are, take a look around you. Everything you have in your life reflects choices you made using your life values as the criteria for your decisions.

Those things you like and enjoy are in alignment with your life values while the things you dislike, detest, or barely tolerate aren't.

Imagine that you're viewing the things you have in your life from the perspective of a stranger. What would a person's likes and dislikes have to be in order to create what you have in your life? What would be important to them? What would they believe? List any descriptive words that come to mind as you visualize the items listed below:

Personal Vehicle

Home

Clothes

Friends

Music

Colors

Using a red pen, highlighter, or crayon, circle the descriptive words which reflect those things you love. Your life values are reflected in these descriptions. Circle any words that describe your dislikes in black. These words are the opposite of your life values. Simply flip them into their reverse meaning and you'll find they have elements of your life values in them.

Compare the words you've circled with the ten most important life values you listed. You should find similarities and perhaps clearer definitions of some of the life values already in your list. You may have even discovered some new ones.

Allow the work you've done so far to settle for a few days and then revisit the list you've created of your ten most important life values. You'll find that when you look at your list again you'll have a new perspective of it. You may be amazed at how accurate it is or you may see some values that you wish to tweak, eliminate, add, or replace. The first version may be perfect or there may be a few more versions of your list before you absolutely know that the values within it are, unquestionably, *your* life values.

Your Very Own Definition of Your Life Values

Webster isn't the only one who can assign meaning to a word. *Everyone* has words that have unique and special meaning for them. For example, "security" can mean very diverse things from one person to the next. For one person it may mean having a loving, nurturing family. For another security may mean having inner strength. There are different types of security, too, such as:

> **Financial security,** which may mean a nine-to-five job for one person, but for another it may mean having a huge savings account. For yet another it may mean a very large line of credit.
> **Spiritual security** may mean being able to pray to the god of one's choice, or it may mean having complete

confidence that the belief one has chosen is the right one for them.

Physical security for one person may mean safety from physical abuse. For another it may mean having a house to live in and food on the table.

In order to use your life values with confidence and clarity in the everyday world, it's important to completely understand what they mean to you. The following exercise will give you the opportunity to do just that.

List your top three core life values and write your own personal definition of what they mean to you. Do this in whatever way works for you — as a dictionary-type definition, as a list of words with similar meanings, as a description of how you know when you are experiencing this value, or any other way that makes sense to you.

1. _____

2. _____

3. _____

Keep these three definitions of your most important life values in a place where you'll be able to see them often during the day in order to reinforce your complete understanding of exactly what your life values mean to you.

So far, you have clearly identified your ten most important life values and have clearly defined the top three so that you clearly understand what they mean to you. Now what?

Live **Your Life Values**

With your life values clearly in mind, you can now begin to live them. When you're living your values, you stay centered and balanced and aren't easily thrown off balance by outward influences, such as other people, your environment, and events.

Making choices based on your values puts you in a power position — not in victim mode. You avoid becoming a victim to the whims of other people, events in your life, and your environment. *You* choose what you'll do, think, and feel in every instance. The power of choice gives you control in your life.

Here's an example. Suppose that the phone rings and it's a client telling you that they no longer require your services. You might choose to think:

> A. "They rejected me", and then choose to feel hurt.
> B. "I must be really bad at what I do", which then contributes to unworthy thoughts and feelings about yourself.
> C. "This is a great opportunity to find out what they liked about my services, what they didn't like, and how I could improve." You may then feel excited about your new growth.

    D. _____

(fill in the blank space with your favorite)

Which of your life values aren't being honored by some of these choices?

How aren't they being honored?

What are some your life values that might be honored in these choices?

How are they being honored?

Living Your Life Values: Part I

For the purpose of helping you understand more clearly how honoring your values makes your life better, let's use a real example from your life.

Think about a situation that you experienced where things weren't going well and you were feeling upset, angry, or frustrated.

Describe in the space below what was happening and be as specific and detailed as possible. Who was involved? Where was it happening? What were you feeling? What were your thoughts? What did you do and what did they do?

Now, go back to your list of core life values. Which of them were not being honored?

Replay

Imagine this situation taking place with one vital difference — now you *are* honoring your life values.

How the situation might evolve differently as you replay it, living your life values?

What are you feeling now about the situation?

Living Your Life Values: Part II

Sometimes you have an experience with someone that goes so smoothly you're amazed at how easily it flowed. "What magical forces were at play?" you might wonder. No need to wonder. The magic was within you. Whether you were aware of it or not, you were honoring your life values.

Think of a real life situation you experienced that ended as a win-win success, but that could have gone the other way to become a

disaster. Think back to your part in the event. What did you say
and do? What was happening?

Which of your life values were you honoring during this
experience?

Your Strengths and Qualities

One of the ways in which your life values influence who you are
is through your inner strengths and qualities. As an example, a
life value of orderliness creates the inner qualities that may
manifest as being immaculate with personal attire, having an
ability to create organization from chaos, and always being on
time.

What are your strengths and qualities? What are you known for
in your circle of friends? In this exercise identify some of your
major inner qualities and strengths, and then connect them to
your life values. You may want to complete this exercise first on
your own, and then do it again later with a friend for additional
insights.

List 10 of your inner qualities and next to each quality note the
life value(s) that it represents.

Quality   Life Value(s)

_____1.

_____

_____2.

_____

_____3.

_____

_____4.

_____

_____5.

_____

_____6.

_____

_____7.

_____

_____8.

_____

_____9.

_____

_____10.

_____

Take a few minutes to review how your inner qualities and strengths reflect your life values and how this is a guidepost to your life purpose.

What themes or patterns do you see? Note them here:

Your Nature Story

Connecting with nature is a grand way to tune in to your deeper self and the wisdom that resides within you. The following exercise may offer some surprises for you.

Take some time to be in nature. Go for a walk in the woods, in a park, or along the beach. Look around and notice all the different elements of nature. Pick something that calls to you — a rock, a tree, an animal, the water. Imagine being it. Really connect with the essence of what you've chosen.

When you feel that you have the essence of whatever you've selected, begin to write about what it's like to *be* this thing.

What new insights were revealed to you in your story?

What new awarenesses do you now have?

Now, go back through your story and circle or highlight words or phrases that represent your life values. Note any that are repeated here:

Do/Think/Feel

Life values are the foundation of the structure that allows you to live your life from the inside out, making your own choices based on what's best for you. Living your life in the opposite direction — from the outside in — puts you in the position of being a victim of outward influences, such as the whims, desires, and needs of other people.

A little practice of *consciously* using your life values will go a long way to make living them as automatic as breathing. For the next week, take a few moments at the end of your day to note which of your life values you used to make a choice or a decision.

Use this format:

My Life Value:_____

What I did:

What I thought:

What I felt:

You may want to continue tracking your use of them even longer than a week in order to record your progress. You might also want to save this record as a future reference to recall how you've successfully used your life values.

Life Values and Your Life Purpose

Consciously filtering your choices through your life values puts you on track to living your life purpose by guiding you to those things which are imortant to you — things that are in alignment with the purposeful work you chose for yourself.

Notes:

Your Personal Boundaries

You've no doubt heard these phrases, or something like them, at one time or another:

> "That's enough of that!"
> "I've stood this as long as I can."
> "I can't take any more of this."
> "That's the last straw."

You may have even been the one saying them. When you hear statements like these coming from another person — or from yourself — it means that a personal boundary has been violated.

Everyone has boundaries. However, few people are aware of them even when they encounter them. Fewer still are aware of their own boundaries. Most people only recognize that they have personal boundaries *after* their boundaries have been violated. Usually the violation had to be quite huge in order to even gain their attention.

Wouldn't it be helpful for you to know what someone's boundaries are *before* you get yelled at for stepping over them? Wouldn't it be even more helpful if others could know what yours are so they can prevent violating them?

And wouldn't it be simply wonderful if *you* know what your boundaries are and how you can prevent others from crossing them?

What Are Personal Boundaries?

Personal boundaries are standards and limits that you set in regard to what you will and will not accept in other people's behavior toward you. They're invisible lines of protection you set around yourself to define what others are allowed or not allowed to do to you or within your presence.

External influences such as events, situations, your environment, time, and other people's desires lose their impact and their power over you when you strengthen and uphold your personal boundaries. Boundaries are part of living your life from the inside out, and this begins with what's most important to you — your life values. When you honor your life values by enforcing your boundaries, you're centered, balanced, and in the place of power — the place where *you* choose what you want to do, think, and feel.

In short, boundaries say, "That's yours. This is mine." This can refer to more than just the physical areas of your life. Boundaries can protect you in many other areas, such as:

> emotional
> mental
> sexual
> piritual
> creative

How Strong Are Your Personal Boundaries?

One easy way to discern if your personal boundaries need to be stronger is to take this quiz. In front of the number for each question, write "Y" for yes and "N" for no.

1. Do other people such as your spouse, co-workers, friends, and family, always seem to be telling you how to live your life?
2. Do people often tell you how easy you are to get along with?
3. Do you suffer from stress related diseases such as high blood pressure, ulcers, fibromyalgia, or eating disorders?
4. Are you often made to feel smaller by other people?
5. Does everybody like you?
6. Do you often find yourself telling other people what they need to do to fix a situation in their lives?
7. Do people sometimes seem to be put off by questions you ask them?
8. Do you often feel that other people take advantage of your kind and generous nature?
9. Are you the one at work who always gets the least desirable assignments?
10. Do you often feel angry after an encounter with another person and aren't exactly sure why?

Give yourself 1 point for every YES answer. Add up your YES answers for your score.

1-3 points: Fairly strong boundaries, although they could use further strengthening.

4-6 points: Your boundaries are a little flabby and need work to get them muscled up.

7-10 points: Your boundaries are 90-pound weaklings! Start *now* to strengthen them!

The Benefits of Strong Personal Boundaries

When you uphold your personal boundaries you have:
- freedom
- inner strength
- balance
- independence
- control of your life
- centeredness
- grounding

How does this happen? How can something as simple as strengthening your personal boundaries have all these powerful effects on your life?

Strong personal boundaries give you CHOICES! When you don't uphold your personal boundaries, you live your life by default. This means that you're giving your power away — your life energy. When you hear someone say things like, "I have to do it" or "I have no choice," what you're hearing is the sound of them giving their personal power away to someone or something else. Personal boundaries put *you* in control with the power of choice. Your personal power is the inner strength you need in order to live your life purpose.

Strong personal boundaries are necessary, mandatory, and imperative to successfully living your life purpose. It's impossible to consciously honor your life values — one of the very most important guideposts to your life purpose — without the support of your personal boundaries. How can you possibly live your purpose if you're living by default, letting other people define you and your life? When you allow this to happen, you're living *their* life, not yours.

You're no longer a victim of other people, events, and your environment. No longer are you pushed and pulled by the whims of outside influences. This is a very important benefit of having and using your personal boundaries. When you honor your life values by upholding your personal boundaries, you're empowered and have control over your life. You have the power to make choices based on what *you* want, instead of being a victim to what other people want. You have the power to implement and activate the most important parts of your life purpose — your values. Without strong personal boundaries you won't be able to honor and protect your life values.

Boundaries set you apart from others and give you a unique identity. They help define who you are and who you are not. Setting strong boundaries is essential to having a healthy life, one in which you're balanced emotionally and mentally. Without strong personal boundaries you're easily thrown off center, tossed around by the needs and desires of other people, in danger of losing your identity and the knowledge of who you truly are.

When you honor your boundaries, you attract people who have a similar sense of self-respect, worth, and esteem. As you uphold your personal boundaries, you broadcast to other people the respect that you have for yourself. When your personal boundaries become stronger, you'll find that the people who disrespect you and drain your energy will be evaporating from your circle of friends and associates. You'll have more energy when you no longer associate with these people because you won't be using your energy to defend your boundaries as often.

Having strong boundaries gives you confidence so that you no longer operate from fear. When you uphold your personal boundaries you gain the ability to remain centered and balanced

31

during any situation. You'll find that you don't succumb to fear as easily nor as readily.

Your communications with others will be more efficient and productive. As you strengthen your personal boundaries you become more clear about your own life values. You'll no longer suffer the confusion or misunderstandings that originate from being unclear about your life values. You'll find that you're in perfect alignment with your values when you uphold your boundaries during your communications. When other people know where you stand, it's easier for them to come forth with their honesty, thus promoting clear communication on both sides. Life is much simpler when you speak from your inner truth.

How Boundaries Relate to Life Values

Personal boundaries are the physical manifestation of life values. They're the powerful vehicles that bring your life values from where they live in your heart and soul out into the world. Boundaries are your life values in action — the ways in which you live your life values. You might think of your life values as nouns and your personal boundaries as the verbs that put the nouns into action.

Some Important Things to Know About Personal Boundaries

1. Know that this is about you. It's not about other people. These are *your* life values and *your* boundaries.

2. Know that it's all about choices. The boundaries you set are *your* choices. How other people choose to react or

respond to you as you uphold your boundaries are their choices. How you feel and what you do are your choices.

3. Know that it's not always possible to say no and have the other person be delighted about it. Expect others to be upset, disappointed, or angry when you inform them of your boundaries. Prepare for it. If it doesn't happen, celebrate!

4. Know that people often don't know that they've violated one of your personal boundaries. People can't be expected to instinctively know what your boundaries are. You must inform them before you can expect compliance from them.

And most important of all:
5. Remember that your personal boundaries are protecting and honoring the most important guideposts you have for your life purpose — your life values.

A Special Note About Abused Children Who Are Now Grown-ups

Children who are raised in an abusive situation, whether it's physical, sexual, or mental, live with relentless personal boundary violation. As helpless little children, they have no power to protect themselves by defending their personal boundaries. Their parents or caretakers teach these unfortunate children nothing about personal boundaries, except that they haven't any.

Most commonly when we think of child abuse, we think of it in a physical context such as sexual molestation, beating, or whipping. However, there are other abusive acts, which are less dramatic yet just as devastating to the health and well being of the child, such as:

- lack of privacy.
- takeover of personal efforts by a parent or older sibling.
- borrowing and use of the child's belongings by others without their permission.
- no voice in the choices that affect them, such as clothes, activities, and friends.
- neglecting to teach the child responsibility by not allowing them to experience the consequences of their actions.

When these children grow up, they became adults on the outside, but inside they're still the defenseless children who know nothing of protecting themselves by means of personal boundaries.

These people have little or no knowledge of personal boundaries — theirs or other people's. As adults they may become shy, scared victims or they may go to the other extreme and become overbearing and intrusive. Both types suffer from a lack of healthy boundaries, even though they're experiencing the imbalance from opposite ends of the scale.

If you are one of these grownup abused children, this information about honoring your personal values may sound alien. *Be gentle with yourself and stay with it.* This learning will prove to be extremely valuable to you. In fact, it may be one of the best things you'll ever do for yourself.

Awareness: The First Step

How do you know when your personal boundaries have been

invaded? At this point you probably aren't aware of your boundaries until they've been grossly violated or totally ignored. Often it may not be until sometime after the fact that you become aware of the boundary infringement.

Certain physical and emotional sensations serve as red alerts, warning you that one of your boundaries is being invaded. There's a variety of ways in which these boundary alerts are experienced, with some of the most common alerts being:

1. **physical discomfort somewhere in your body,** such as a sensation of being punched in the stomach or having the wind knocked out of you. Tenseness anywhere in your body, such as in your neck or jaw muscles is another common boundary alert. Common sayings such as, "I felt like I'd been kicked in the gut," or "It knocked the wind out of me," or "That just torques my jaws." are all responses to boundary invasions.

2. **sudden or growing anger** during an interaction with another person. The awareness of this alert may not happen until some time has passed after the interchange. This is very common with people who are not yet cognizant of their personal boundaries.

3. **a feeling of being made smaller or diminished by another person.** This reaction is often accompanied by a change in physiology, such as hunching the shoulders, curling up in a slouch, or collapsing the torso in an instinctive effort to protect their most vulnerable parts from being harmed.

4. **feeling shocked or stunned by the actions of another.**

5. **wanting to step backward,** away from another person or to escape from their presence.

Becoming Aware of Your Boundary Alerts

Gaining awareness of how you sense boundary invasion and identifying your personal boundary alerts are the first steps to building a healthy set of personal boundaries. The best way to gain this awareness is to revisit how you felt when you were having experiences that you suspect were boundary violations.

Think back to an experience you've had that left you feeling angry or frustrated with someone, and which you now suspect was a violation of your personal boundaries. What did you sense or feel as it was happening? After it happened? How did you react? These sensations, no matter how insignificant you may deem them to be, are your boundary alerts. List *all* of your feelings, both physical and emotional, here:

1.

2.

3.

4.

5.

Repeat this exercise four more times using different experiences, noticing any trends in how you experience boundary invasion. For one week, practice noticing these symptoms of boundary invasion. Do nothing beyond simply noticing how you feel as you sense your boundary alerts. You may want to make notes of these feelings or journal about them in order to become even more clear about how your particular boundary alerts feel.

Continue this practice until you're familiar with the sensations of your personal boundary alerts and you feel fairly comfortable that you can quickly recognize when your boundaries are being infringed upon.

If this is foreign territory to you, as it is with many people, you may not notice your boundary alerts until some time after your boundary has been violated. That's okay. You didn't walk the first time you tried, either.

Be kind to yourself and give yourself a pat on the back each time you notice one of your boundary alerts. The more you practice, the sooner you'll begin to become aware of the boundary invasion, until there's no time lag at all between the invasion and your recognition of it.

Tracking the Cause of the Boundary Alert

After you've become familiar with how your boundary alerts feel to you, you're ready to practice discerning their causes.

During the next week, whenever you become aware of a boundary invasion, briefly note the circumstances, your boundary alert, and the life values that were not being honored.

You can use the space provided here or keep a separate journal.

1.

2.

3.

4.

5.

6.

7.

8.

9.

10.

Becoming aware that you're experiencing violation of your personal boundaries is an important step to living an empowered life — a life of *your* choice.

Once you feel confident that you can quickly recognize a personal boundary invasion and can also identify the life value that is not being honored, you're ready to defend your boundaries.

Upholding Your Personal Boundaries

There are three basic steps to upholding your boundaries:

> 1. Inform the violator of your personal boundary and, if appropriate, the life value that it honors. State it in a calm voice. Don't be angry, defensive, or sc-sc-sc-scared.
> 2. Ask the violator to honor your boundary.
> 3. Thank them.

Sounds quite simple, doesn't it? However, at first it might be intimidating to state your boundary to someone, especially if they've been getting away with pushing you around for a considerable amount of time. Just remember this: they won't respect you if they can push you around. When you allow others to disrespect you and tell you what to do, you've lost the right of choice in your life, which means that you've also lost control over your life. When this happens you're living someone else's life and are definitely *not* living *your* life purpose.

As you practice — and you'll have lots of practice before you begin upholding your personal boundaries out in the real world — it will become easier and less intimidating. Plus, the rewards you reap are ten times greater than any discomfort you might experience as you begin to uphold your boundaries. You'll begin to experience confidence, inner strength, calmness, balance, and peace. The most important reward you'll gain is much more than these. You'll gain *your* life. No longer will you be directed by other people. You'll have *choice* in what you do.

You may get a variety of reactions from people when you first begin to uphold your life values with your personal boundaries. Surprise, shock, and anger are a few of the responses that you may experience from your boundary invaders. After all, these people have been getting away with their disrespectful, dishonoring behavior toward you for a long time. They may not be exactly elated at losing control over you.

When you get a reaction that's less than what you desire when you uphold your personal boundary, you need to remember the following:

- don't justify, rationalize, or apologize for your boundary.
- don't open it up to debate.
- don't fill in any stunned silences with an explanation as to why you're doing this.

Justifications, explanations, and apologies defuse the power of your boundaries, and may even render them worthless. A simply worded statement of what your boundary is, how you want the violator to honor it, and a gracious "thank you" are all that's required to defend your boundary.

Almost always the other person is aware that they were trespassing, knows that they have been doing so for some time, and is simply amazed that you finally got the courage to speak your truth. They may get a little pouty because their game is over now, but in the long run you'll gain one of two very big benefits: either they'll respect you and will stop pushing you around, or they'll go away. If they choose the latter, they have blessed you with two *immense* favors:

1. They've relieved you of their energy-draining behavior.
2. They've created space for a new person who respects you to enter your life.

There's always the possibility that you might get a big surprise in the form of happy compliance from the boundary infringer, almost as if they've just been waiting for you to stand up for yourself. In fact, the majority of my clients who have begun to uphold their personal boundaries with family members have reported grand successes. Family is often the most difficult to deal with because there seems to be a belief that people can do things to each other within a family that they'd never think of doing to their friends and associates. The fact that most of my clients begin with their family members when learning to uphold their boundaries *and* are reporting great successes is encouraging news for all beginners of this practice.

One client's experience involved her teenage daughter who was not acting respectful during conversations with her mother. One day, her mother gathered her courage and told her daughter that one of her most important life values was respect and that she required her daughter to be respectful to her during their conversations. The daughter stopped her verbal abuse almost mid-word. She then apologized to her mother and they re-started the conversation on a much more respectful tone. My client reported that she hadn't had such a wonderful, productive conversation with her daughter in years.

Extreme Reactions

On rare occasions, you may experience extreme reactions from boundary violators. If they get angry, start to argue with you, or yell at you, walk away. **If they start to get physically abusive, PUT AS MUCH DISTANCE AS YOU CAN BETWEEN YOU AND THEM AND DO IT AS FAST AS YOU CAN.**

You do not deserve to suffer from this type of behavior. You deserve respectful, honest, and honorable behavior from others. If they are not capable of that, escape their presence as quickly as is humanly possible.

People who are all steamed up are certainly not going to listen to reason. At this point there is nothing else you can do but preserve yourself. You've done as much as you can simply by informing them that their behavior is no longer acceptable to you. If the situation is critical, enlist the aid of appropriate professionals.

What Are *Your* Personal Boundaries?

Your values spring to life when you honor them with a personal boundary. Without the activation of personal boundaries, your life values are just invisible thoughts in your head. Personal boundaries breathe life into them and bring them into physical reality. Some examples:

- A woman who has a life value of privacy manifests this value when she doesn't allow anyone to use her computer.

- Another woman whose life value is freedom won't be tied down to a job with regular hours inside a building. She has her own business, which allows her complete freedom of choice about when and where she will work.

- A man who has a life value of security avoids the stock market and places his investments in insured, interest bearing accounts at an accredited financial institution.

List your top three life values in the space provided and beneath them, write three personal boundaries that honor these values. Begin the statement with "I won't allow…" or "I must have…"

Value:_____

Value:_____

Value: _____

The Language of Personal Boundaries

Knowing *how* to say something is as important as knowing *what* to say. There are many ways to say almost everything but not all of them will get you the response you want. A good example probably is one of your boundaries exactly as you wrote it in the last exercise. Imagine saying it to someone. Chances are you wouldn't get agreeable compliance if you stated it exactly in the way you just wrote it.

Now that you have a basic framework of your personal boundaries for your top three life values, you can craft verbiage for them, transforming them into language that will be heard and accepted by whomever is violating your boundary. The odds of getting someone to stop doing an unacceptable behavior just by telling them to stop are minimal. The odds increase in your favor when you explain why it's important to you. And the odds skyrocket straight up when you use a certain word.

That word is **honor.**

When you ask someone to *honor* your request, you're asking them to do more than just stop their annoying or disrespectful behavior. You're offering them the opportunity to *become* honorable. You're not asking them to do something for you. Instead, you're asking them to do something that will make them an honorable person. What a graceful way to request respect for your personal boundary. Who could resist?

Below are a few examples of ways to state your personal boundaries. Notice that they follow the three-step formula of informing the boundary invader, asking for compliance, and thanking them.

"_____ is very important to me and I do not allow anyone to _____ _____ in my presence. I ask you to honor this. Thank you."

"_____ is one of the values that I live my life by. To honor my value I do not allow anyone to _____ _____ in my presence. I ask that you honor my value. Thank you."

"_____ is one of my most important life values. I require _____ _____ in order for you honor my value. Thank you."

"One of my most important life values is _____ It's how I choose to live my life. I ask you to honor my value by

_____. Thank you."

Notice that in each of these examples the word "honor" was used. This very powerful word changes an everyday request into one that will make the boundary invader feel like a better person, an honorable person, if they simply comply with your request. And in actuality, they *will* become a better person for honoring and respecting your life value.

Feel free to play with these examples, rearranging and changing the language so that you're comfortable using them. Practice saying these personal boundary requests daily, in private or to someone you trust and are comfortable with.

When you're comfortable with the language, informing others of your personal boundaries becomes so much easier. Then as it becomes time to state your boundary, you won't be searching for the words — or worse, unable to speak at all because you don't know what to say. Also, when you know how to say it in a way that will be heard and received by the boundary invader, you increase your chances of getting agreement and compliance.

It's Showtime!

When you've practiced verbalizing your personal boundaries enough that you feel comfortable as you say them, you're ready to try them out in real life.

If there is someone you know who repeatedly violates your boundary in the same way each time, you have the advantage of being able to prepare your boundary language beforehand. If, however, you seem to experience boundary invasions of all different sorts and from a variety of people, you may want to uphold your boundary in two parts. This method gives you time to accurately identify the life value being dishonored *and* to create the verbiage for your boundary so that you'll be comfortable stating it to the violator.

> **Part One:** When you become aware of the boundary violation by noticing one of your boundary alerts, excuse yourself from the violator's presence. You might ask for time out, announce that you need to go to the bathroom, or use any ploy that will remove you from their presence. When you have some private time, review what was happening and discern the life value that was not being honored.

> **Part two:** Create a personal boundary that will honor this life value. Write it down. Practice it. Then, pick a time and present it to the violator.

As you become more adept at upholding your personal boundaries, you'll find that you probably won't need two-part process. The identification of your life values and how they're not being honored will become almost second nature for you and this time lag will disappear.

This two-part process worked with success for one client. She wanted to invite some friends to go for a sail on the boat that she and her husband owned. She wished also to provide sandwiches and drinks for them. It was important to her because it honored her life value of community. Her husband, who is extremely frugal, objected to her supplying the food and drinks. They ended the discussion in an argument with him forbidding her to make sandwiches for her friends.

At this point, she recognized she was experiencing one of her boundary alerts — a feeling of having the wind knocked out of her. So she retreated for a time out, reviewed her life values, discerned which of them was not being honored, and created the verbiage for a boundary.

She returned to her husband and voiced her boundary, including the part about which of her values it honored. He looked at her for a moment, then asked her why she hadn't previously told him how important it was and why it mattered so much to her. They went to the store together and bought the food. He even helped her prepare it. They had a wonderful sailing experience with their friends and really enjoyed the food they'd prepared together.

What I Did and How I Felt

One of the best methods for identifying and reinforcing the habit of honoring life values by upholding personal boundaries is to keep track of what you did and how you felt about it. Take a few minutes at the end of each day to note each time you acted with integrity of your life values by honoring it with a personal boundary and how you felt about it. Use this format:

Date:
What I Did:

How I Felt:

Incoming and Outgoing Boundaries

Boundaries work two ways. So far the focus has been on outgoing boundaries — the boundaries *you* set to protect yourself. After focusing so intently on your own personal boundaries it can come as quite a surprise to realize that other people have boundaries too.

As you work on strengthening your own boundaries, you'll become more aware of other people's boundaries. This has the benefit of increasing the respect in your relationships with others — both the respect that others have for you and the respect you have for them. The end result is that *all* of your relationships, whether personal or business, will be on a much higher level as you both honor each other's values.

Communicate openly about the work you're doing regarding your life values and personal boundaries with people you believe to be safe. This may open them up to communicating *their* personal boundaries to you. With everything out in the open, honoring their personal boundaries becomes a snap.

Not everyone will be so open, willing, and compliant. Other people may not be as available with their boundaries as you are. This can make the task of recognizing other people's personal boundaries a bit difficult, especially when you're quite new to them yourself.

The solution to this problem is simple — when in doubt, ask. Most people won't be offended when you ask them if you've just inadvertently stepped out of bounds. In fact, most people are relieved when asked about their personal boundaries, and are often grateful when the violator is considerate and aware enough to sense they've trespassed.

The important point is that you continue to work on honoring your life values by strengthening your personal boundaries. Your boundaries get stronger and easier to uphold each time you use them. You'll notice that as they become stronger, not only will your life become of a higher quality, you'll find the path to living your life purpose will be much smoother and easier to travel.

Notes:

Discovering Your Life Purpose

As you evolved from a child to an adult, your life path took many twists and turns, detoured around many obstacles, and may have even hit a few cul-de-sacs from time to time. The result is that you've been nudged off track and now you're not truly living your life purpose.

You're not alone. In fact, you're a part of the vast majority. Most of the humans walking around today have forgotten what they came to this planet to do. You may have a very full and busy life, but still have a deep sense of knowing that something is missing… something vitally important. You know something's lacking, and without it your life feels incomplete, unsatisfying, and without meaning.

Your feeling of dissatisfaction and your thoughts that something vital is lacking in your life are messages from your soul. It's gently nudging you to get back on the right path. Your search has led you to this book; the fact that you're reading these words signifies that you are most assuredly ready to begin your inner journey and begin living your life purpose.

51

You may have remembered some of the purpose you chose for this lifetime — just enough perhaps to find a job or career that incorporates some of the elements of the important work you chose to do. Still, you have a strong inner knowing that there's more, and the feeling won't go away. The dissatisfaction you feel and the sense you have that there's still something very important missing from your life are telling you that you still haven't hit the sweet spot of living your life purpose.

There are a lucky few who are now fully living their life purpose. You can recognize them by their high energy, happy outlook, excitement about their life, and passion for what they're doing. This group of people is growing like a snowball rolling down a steep mountainside, as more and more people remember their life purpose and take back their power. They feel satisfaction that is soul deep as they do the work they chose — work that allows them to be of service to others in their own unique way, as they joyfully fulfill their Soul Contract.

Now it's time for you to live *your* life purpose.

But what if you don't remember what it is?

That's why you have been guided to this book. It's not just a coincidence that you're reading this now. You see, you've set up clues that are almost infallible to guide you back to your true path.

Some of these clues may seem to be simply synchronistic events. They're not. These "coincidences", such as finding a book with just the information you're looking for or meeting just the right person, were all planned by *you* before you were birthed onto this planet. These are the clues that you set up for yourself.

In the movie *Total Recall*, Arnold Schwarzennegger played a character who knows he'll be going through a process in which he'll lose all memory of his true identity. To overcome this obstacle, he sets up clues for himself which he'll be able to find in his future. These clues lead him to remember who he is, and he goes on to save the world... in this case Mars. You, like Arnold's character, set up clues which you could find in *your* future so you can remember your true identity *and* the work you desire to do in order to be of the highest service to others.

During this chapter, you'll find a series of fun exercises that will take you back to a time before you had layers of programming piled on you by others as you grew up. You'll return to a time when you still remembered your life purpose... to the time when you were a young child.

As you peel away the layers of social, familial, and environmental programming that you've acquired throughout your life, the true essence of your life purpose will be revealed to you. You may be surprised at the results you get! Often, as you do the work, it may seem so familiar that you may feel like you're going home again.

Remembering Your Life Purpose

When you were a very young child you were in your purest form — un-adult-erated, so to speak. You hadn't taken on any of the programming from outside influences such as other people, the many forms of media, and school systems. During this period of your life you still remembered your life purpose.

Major clues about the nature of your life purpose lie in what you loved to do when you were a young child. You may think that you were just having fun being a kid and playing at what you loved most. In reality, you were acting out your life purpose. Ask anyone who feels fulfilled with the work they're doing now to tell you what they loved doing best when they were a kid, and they'll talk about how they loved to play at some form of what they're now doing. Some examples are:

- A woman who loved to play with fabric and colors as a child now creates and sells beautiful hand-painted silk scarves.
- Another was always playing with animals of some sort — pets, bugs, snakes. Today she runs a very busy dog sitting service and her clients, both human and canine, are delighted with the care she loves to lavish on them.
- A man who voraciously read about travel and foreign lands in his childhood loves the work he does now as a cross-country truck driver.

So sit back and make yourself comfortable, relax, and get ready to begin the journey of discovering your life purpose.

Through the Ages

Let your mind go backward in time to when you were a very young child — five years of age or younger. Envision yourself playing at your favorite activity, something you loved to do whenever you had the chance or were given the choice.

Describe what you were doing:

What did you like most about it?

Why was it important to you?

Come forward in time to when you were between the ages of six and eight years. What was your favorite playtime activity at this age? Your favorite toys? Friends? Where did you play most often?

What did you like most about it?

Why was that important to you?

Now come forward in time to when you were between the ages of nine and eleven years. What was your favorite playtime activity then? When you were playing, what did you like to do most of all?

What did you like most about it?

Why was it important to you?

Now, once more, come forward in time until the time when you were about the ages of 12 to 15. When you were playing, what did you like to do most of all? Who were you with? Where were you?

What did you like most about it?

Why was it important to you?

What are the similarities, patterns, or repeated notations in each of the ages that you've written about?

Which of your life values are reflected?

Write down any additional insights that you gained from this exercise.

What is the most predominant and recurring theme you uncovered during this exercise?

How does the essence of this theme appear in your life now?

Your Fabulous Career

The purpose of the previous exercise is to distill the passions that you had when you were a child — free from the "shoulds" that were layered upon you as you grew into adulthood. Now that you've identified the essence of your life purpose, you'll get to play with it and create your fabulous career.

This exercise will be more effective for you if you enlist the aid of someone, like a friend or your life coach, to take notes so that you can let your imagination run freely. You'll need three sheets of paper plus additional paper for note taking. On one sheet of paper write in **BIG BOLD LETTERS** the following: **IN MY 20s**. On the second sheet write: **IN MY 40s**, and on the last one write: **ALMOST RETIRED**. Spread these sheets of paper on the floor. They hold the space and the energy of where you were and what you were doing during the times written on them.

If you haven't yet gotten to the period of your life that's written on the paper, don't fret. This exercise isn't about what was — it's about what might be. You're going to be playing with what you loved to do as a child and bring it forward in time, using your imagination to create a career out of one of your favorite playtime activities.

You may want to enlist the help of a friend or your life coach to take notes for you. This will enable you to flow with your creativity because you won't have to stop to write down your thoughts before you forget them.

To begin, select one of your favorite things you liked to do when you were a child. Then, holding the memory of that playtime activity, step on the first piece of paper marked **IN MY 20s**. Close your eyes and imagine that you're actually in your twenties and you now have a career that involves doing that thing you loved to do as a child. Describe your fabulous career as if you are currently doing it, letting yourself be limitless and imaginative to the max. Have fun with this exercise and freely use your imagination. Be as illogical, frivolous, irreverent, unrealistic, silly, outrageous, and unbounded as your inner child wants you to be.

What do you absolutely looooove about this career?

What are the essences of it that make it so wonderful for you?

Which of your life values are reflected in this work?

Now step onto the second piece of paper marked **IN MY 40s**. Imagine that you actually *are* in your forties. How has your fabulous career evolved? What does it look like now? Remember to release your imagination to play and be free. This is pretend.

What are the things about this career that you love the most?

Which of your life values are reflected in your career now?

When you step onto the last piece of paper on which you've written **ALMOST RETIRED**, imagine that you're approaching retirement in your fabulous career, whatever age that might be.

How has your career evolved? What wonderful form has your work taken?

What do you love most about it? What's most important to you about the work you're doing?

Which of your life values are reflected in your career now?

As you look back over your fabulous career and the three ages at which you took pause, what jumps out at you as most important about it?

During your entire fabulous career, what did you love most about it?

Which of your life values have been reflected throughout your entire fabulous career?

If you'd like deeper insights, more proof, or if you just want to have more fun, repeat this exercise using any of the things you loved to do as a child. As you transform them into your fabulous career you're actually expanding upon the essence of them, which allows you to more easily see them for what they really are — very important clues about your life purpose. The more often you do it, the more clues you'll have with which to discover your life purpose.

Backing Into Your Future

Often, when you most want something and are going after it, whatever you want eludes you. It seems as if the harder you run after it, the more you're chasing it away from you.

This phenomenon is exemplified in an incident that happened when I was preparing to ride horses with a friend. She had a horse that was almost impossible to catch and, of course, that was the one she chose for me. With both of my jacket pockets packed full of grain, I grabbed the halter and went with my friend out to the pasture to catch our horses.

When my horse saw me coming at him with my hand full of grain and the dreaded halter, he casually walked away from me. I picked up my pace and so did he. I stopped and so did he. Although I think the horse was enjoying it, this dance between us was becoming rather frustrating for me. Then inspiration hit. I turned around with my back to him and began walking backwards. The horse just stood there, thinking that as long as my back was toward him he was safe. Horse logic said that even if my feet were moving, they must be taking me away from him. He was one surprised horse when I got next to him, spun around, and threw the halter rope around his neck! I could almost hear him thinking, "Now, how the heck did she do that?"

Chasing after something you want, such as your life purpose, can be a lot like catching that wary horse. As long as it sees you coming, it will continue to be elusively just out of reach. Sometimes you just have to back into it.

The ways in which you were programmed while you were growing up have much to do with whether you walk directly up to your desires, or whether you'll have to back into them. If you were raised like most children, you were innocently, lovingly, and incorrectly taught to deny your true passions in the mistaken belief that this would keep you from becoming arrogant, selfish, and egotistical. How often did you hear one of your parents or your teachers say to you, "Oh, you don't want *that*. It's not good for you. You want this instead." You knew what you wanted, didn't you? But the only person who would listen to you was yourself. So your inner dialog was all about you knowing what you wanted and that you didn't want the other thing that someone was trying to foist on you. You accepted it anyway so you'd be a "good little child."

Now that you're an adult that polite little child is still inside you and you have a lifelong habit of identifying what you *don't* want. It's much easier for you to know what you *don't* want than to know what you *do* want. So, in order to find out what you truly want, you may just have to back into it by first defining what you don't want.

Your wants, desires, and passions are hugely important clues about your life purpose. By defining what you don't want you'll be backing into yet another vital clue to help you identify your life purpose.

The Job From Hell

In this exercise, describe your version of the job from hell. This is an opportunity for you to get absolutely clear about all the things you *don't* want to have as you do your work. Describe every detail about your job from hell. What is your work environment? Do you have co-workers? If so, what are they like? Do you have a boss? What's your boss like? Make note of sights, sounds, smells, and any other sensations you can think of. What hours do you work? Do you work in one location or do you move from location to location? Get as descriptive and detailed as you can, and make it as baaaaaad as you possibly can.

The Worst of the Worst

Go back through your job from hell description and circle or highlight all the words and phrases that stand out for you — all the worst of the worst. List them here:

Use additional paper or a notebook if you need more room.

Next to each word or phrase, note your life values which are not being honored or are lacking. Are there any patterns or repeated themes? Describe them here:

Your Perfect Work

What you want is the opposite of what you don't want. This may seem simplistic, but it's a very important bit of logic that often gets overlooked or ignored because it *is* so extremely simple.

The next step in backing into discovering your desires is to transpose what you don't want into what you do want. Simple. For instance, if your job from hell includes working a 9 to 5 job in the city, the opposite of that might be freelancing from your home in the country or being a consultant and flying to your clients' locations all over the world.

Take each item from the Worst of the Worst list and turn it into whatever the opposite might be for you. If you come up with multiple options, note them all. Play with this exercise and have fun! Free your imagination and get as creative and limitless as you want.

1.
2.
3.
4.
5.
6.
7.
8.
9.
10.

Next to each of the items, note which of your life values is being honored or reflected. What are the patterns or repeated themes?

Are any of the elements in the job from hell and your perfect work exercises in your life now? If so, describe how they appear in your life:

The Bottom Line

Bottom lining can often bring clarification in a manner that's all soooo simple. Complete this sentence:

Whether I get paid for it or not, what I love to do most of all now is:

Mind Mapping

A mind map is a unique tool that can be used for many purposes including organizing information, brainstorming, making choices, and creating a plan. Mind maps are valuable tools for gaining more clarity about your life purpose and they're fun to create. It's easy to use a mind map. It can be done quickly and simply or in a complex and elaborate style.

To begin a mind map, draw a circle or some other shape, such as a heart, square, or diamond, in the center of a large sheet of paper. Then place a word or a picture in it — something that represents the main theme of the map, such as your life purpose. As a word comes to mind that defines, describes, or is a part of the main theme of the map, draw a line radiating outward from the shape and write this word on it. More words will pop into your head that further define or describe the first word; when they do, draw another line attached to the first line and add the word on the new line. As new thoughts appear in your mind, attach them either to an existing line or begin a new one from the center — which ever is appropriate.

Each new line that begins from the center is a main branch, describing a different aspect of the subject of your mind map. Your map will grow outward in a radius as you add lines to the main theme, and then add lines to those lines and so on. Remember, each line that's added further defines or describes the line it's attached to.

For example, if the theme of your mind map is "teaching a class" some of the branches may be "content", "advertising", and "location". Subsidiary branches on the "location" branch might be "free", "under $100", "over $100", ">50 miles", and "<50 miles". Specific locations might be listed under each subcategory, or additional defining words might be added.

For brainstorming and creative mind maps it helps to work as quickly as possible so that your inner critic doesn't take over. Each inner critic uses a favorite trick to distract you and stop your progress as it tries to make unimportant details seem important. If you have a sudden urge to make sure every word is spelled correctly or find yourself questioning whether to use a hyphen or not, take a few seconds to tell your inner critic to kindly shut up so that you can continue the important work of creating your mind map. Then resume working as rapidly as you can.
You can use the space below to practice creating a mind map. Then when you feel like you have the hang of it, use a much larger piece of paper — at least poster size — to allow yourself more room to explore your passions, interests, likes, dislikes and all the wondrous things that will lead you to greater understanding of your life purpose.

Begin now by drawing a heart in the center of the next page and then writing the theme of your "practice" mind map inside the heart... and have fun!

Completing Your Life Purpose Mind Map

The two most difficult phases of creation are starting and stopping. How do you know when your mind map is complete and it's time to stop? You may simply feel that you have nothing left to add to it or you may just have a sense of it being complete. On the other hand, you may find yourself so drawn into the process that you feel like you could continue forever and may even lose track of time. If this is the case, you might want to set a time limit for the creation of your mind map.

When you're done with your mind map observe it from an overall viewpoint. What stands out for you? What do you notice most about it?

Now look at these words you've just written. Circle or highlight any that are important, stand out for you, or are repeated. Which of your life values are represented in your mind map?

Keep your mind map handy by posting it on the wall of your office or any other place where you spend time so that you can add information as it occurs to you.

You'll also be using your mind map later when you begin to create your plan for living your life purpose.

The Work You're Doing Now

You may feel like the work you're doing now isn't big enough, important enough, or that it has no purpose or meaning, so it can't *possibly* be your life purpose. Know this: there are many levels and varieties of living your life purpose. You simply don't recognize them as such, yet. As you progress through *An Inner Journey* you may discover that many elements of your life purpose exist for you right now.

The work you're doing now in order to pay your bills may have higher aspects related to your life purpose. They're just so deeply hidden or well camouflaged that you don't recognize them.

This exercise will assist you in uncovering just what those higher aspects of your current work might be. Complete the following:

The work I'm doing now includes the following tasks, chores, and responsibilities:

1.

2.

3.

4.

5.

What I like about this work is:

1.

2.

3.

4.

5.

What I do *not* like about this work:

1.

2.

3.

4.

5.

If you have more descriptions, likes, and dislikes about your work, continue on another sheet of paper.

The items on these lists are important clues about how you're currently living — or not living — forms of your life purpose. This will become more clear in the next exercise.

The Energy Exchange

That which you enjoy gives you energy and that which you dislike drains your energy. Even thinking about these items will have an effect upon your energy level. Whatever gives you energy is a clue to your passions, which are clues to your life purpose. Whatever drains your energy is a clue to what your life purpose *isn't*.

Not only is your energy level an important clue about the nature of your life purpose work, it's vital information for you as you go about your daily existence. If everything you're doing is an energy drain, it won't be long before you have no life force left and won't have the energy required to explore your life purpose work, let alone actually do the work.

Using the previous list of what you like about your current work, identify what about this work gives you energy. After each item rate the amount of energy you receive from it on a scale from one to ten, with one being a dead battery and ten being high voltage.

1.

2.

3.

4.

5.

Using the list of what you dislike about your work, identify exactly what part of it drains your energy. Rate how much energy you give to this aspect of your work using a scale of one to ten with ten being the maximum energy drain.

1.

2.

3.

4.

5.

How does the energy balance out betweeen your likes and dislikes?

What gives you the most energy?

What drains your energy the most?

What is the opposite of those things that drain your energy?

Which of your life values are honored in the work that gives you energy

Which are dishonored in the energy draining work?

Distilling The Essence of Your Life Purpose

You may be wondering when you're going to get to the juicy stuff and clearly define your life purpose. A precise definition restricts creativity and reduces the array of options you have for manifesting your purposeful work. Rather than limiting the opportunities available to you by exactly defining your life purpose, what you'll do now is summarize the clues you've uncovered, distilling them until you have the essence of your life purpose work.

This essence is like a multi-purpose magic wand, giving you the power to do the following:

- create your life purpose work in a myriad of forms, shapes, and styles.
- illuminate the elements of your life purpose that already exist for you.
- empower yourself to make choices in alignment with your life purpose.

Refer to the exercises you've already completed in this chapter to put all the clues into one pot so that you can easily distill them into the essence of your life purpose.

Exercise: Through The Ages

The one thing you loved to do most as a child was:

What you loved most about it was:

The life value(s) that it reflects is:

Exercise: Your Fabulous Career

What you love most about your fabulous career is:

Which of your life values is reflected in this work?

Exercise: The Job From Hell

What are your top five worst of the worst things about this job?

1.

2.

3.

4.

5.

Which of your life values are not being honored?

Exercise: Your Perfect Work

What are your top five best of the best things about this job?
1.

2.

3.

4.

5.

Which of your life values are honored with this work?

Exercise: Mind Mapping

What are the most important words that you circled or highlighted on your mind map?

Which of your life values do they represent?

Exercise: The Work You're Doing Now

What is the most important thing that you like about the work you are doing now?

What's the opposite of the thing you dislike most about your work now?

Exercise: The Energy Exchange

What one thing gives you the most energy in your current work?

Which of your life values are honored in this work?

The Finale: Summarizing the Summary

Go through the summaries above and list the life values that you've written in each of them. Each time a life value is repeated place a hash mark (/) after it.

It should be fairly easy for you to see which life values are most important to you, and which of them you absolutely *must* have in your work. These values are most important clues you have to direct you toward living your life purpose.

Now, go through the summary again and list the words and phrases that are other than your life values. Again, if there are any repeats, use a hash mark for each repetition.

Complete these sentences using the life values and other words that you noted most often:

The three most important life values that *must* be honored in my work *without exception* are
1.

2.

3.

The three most important things I *must* have in my work in order to feel fulfilled and satisfied are:
1.

2.

3.

The essence of your life purpose is the combination of your most important life values and the three things you absolutely must have in your work.

This essence is the magic wand that will allow you to create your life purpose work. Use these vitally important clues that comprise this essence to guide you day-by-day, moment-by-moment, in all the choices you make. This process insures that your choices will be conscious choices moving you *toward* living your life purpose. With these clues brought to light, you can illuminate all areas in your life in which you're already living your life purpose so you can enhance those aspects even more.

Notes:

Creating Your Plan

Congratulations! You've already come a long way on your inner journey of living your life purpose.

- You identified your core life values — one of the most important clues to your life purpose — and explored how they impact every aspect of your life.
- You learned about your personal boundaries — what they are, how to strengthen them, and how to use them to honor and support your life values.
- You uncovered the clues you created for yourself and distilled them into the essence of your life purpose.

The next step is to transform all the mental, emotional, and spiritual work you've done up to this point into physical reality. It's not going to do you or anyone else much good if all you do is *think* about living your life purpose. Remember... your life purpose is the work you chose to do this lifetime in order to be of service to others. You can only be of service by moving into action and actually *doing* the work of your life purpose.

Now it's time for you to begin the process of bringing the essence of your life purpose from your inner world into your outer world by creating your plan. Whether you're creating a plan for your journey into living your life purpose or a trip you've chosen for a vacation, the process is the same:

- First you do the research. For your vacation this might mean looking at brochures, consulting a travel agent, or perusing travel magazines. For the journey of living your life purpose, the research is to identify the clues you left for yourself, such as your life values and what you loved to do as a child.
- Next, based on the findings of your research, you decide where you want to go and what you want to do. For your inner journey, this is the process of distilling the clues into the essence of your life purpose.
- Then you plan how you're going to get there. This is where you are now in the process of living your life purpose.
- Finally, you step into action and go on your trip. This part of your inner journey comes a bit later.

Every journey — whether a business trip, a vacation, or the journey of living your life purpose — is a unique experience. There are many variables, some of which are chosen and some which are completely unexpected. The route you take, the vehicles you choose, the time you spend at each stop en route, and what you do when you arrive, are just some of the variables that are a part of traveling. You may choose a direct route for part of your journey. At other times you may want a route that allows you to meander along and wander wherever you feel drawn.

With so many routes to get to any given destination, how do you know which one is the best for you? During this chapter you'll explore several different planning systems and tools for your use as you travel on your journey of living your life purpose.

The Map Is Not the Territory

It may all look good on paper, but when the time comes for you to actually travel on your chosen path, your map may not look anything like the territory. There may be cul de sacs, detours, washouts, and potholes that don't show up on your map. Any of these can instantly rearrange your carefully planned journey. As you continue past these challenges you'll find that they offer opportunities for you to gain greater knowledge about your journey. Just as an unexpected turn of events during a trip can lead to opportunities for learning more about the people and places where you're traveling, the unexpected experiences you'll have during your life purpose journey offer much wisdom to smooth your journey ahead.

Flexibility is a key concept to keep in mind, not only as you create your plans but afterward, as you're actually experiencing the implementation of your plans. Know that no matter how careful you are in creating your plans and how detailed they may be, life happens. We'll go into this further later when we delve into what stops you. For now, simply understand that making a plan is important *and* that it's just as important to make allowances for the unexpected.

Creating Your Map

The biggest difference between a trip to Florida and the inner journey of living your life purpose is that there's already a map showing you how to get to Florida. When you begin the journey of living your life purpose, you're stepping into unmapped territory.

The good news is that you get to create your own map to guide you from where you are now to where you want to be — living your life purpose. *You* are the cartographer. It's your map and you can create it any way you wish.

You already have one marvelous tool for creating your map. In the previous chapter, you learned about mind maps and how to use them as creative tools to explore the form of your life purpose. Now you get to use a mind map again — this time as a planning tool.

If you have an aptitude for technology, you can go to the mind map website and download the free trial computer program at www.mindmap.com. It creates a mind map automatically as you insert the information.

If you'd rather be more hands-on, you can begin by gathering all the tools you'll want to use: colored pens or crayons, pictures, yarn, glitter, and other fun materials. Use a large piece of paper; poster size is good. Mind maps have a way of growing until they've become quite huge.

Once you have all your materials together, prepare to connect with your creative self. Get comfortable and take a slow, deep, relaxing breath or two. State out loud that your intent in creating this mind map is to discover a multitude of ways in which to live your life purpose.

Remember to begin your mind map at the center of the paper by inserting the theme or focus of your mind map and then radiating lines outward. The first lines are the main themes or most important aspects of your life purpose. Each line you add with a word or image on it will enhance, define, or give more information about the line it's attached to.

Have fun with this process and let your imagination flow. This is not a test and there are no wrong answers. *Everything* is allowed! Add anything that comes into your head to your mind map, no matter how silly or irrelevant you may think it is at the time. Something may pop into your head and you might want to dismiss as not being important. Add it to your mind map anyway. As you play with it, that silly thing may grow and transform into a wonderful way for you to begin living your life purpose.

Now, begin, starting at the center of the paper.

When an hour has passed, or when you feel complete with your mind map (whichever comes first), stop. Take a few moments to review it and notice anything that seems to stand out.

What new options do you now realize? What new ideas, concepts, and opportunities do you see?

What else did you gain from creating this mind map?

How did your life values show up?

Keep your mind map in a place where you can view it during the day. As you spend time with it, additional ideas may come to you. Feel free to add to your mind map anytime.

Now that you know how to construct a mind map, you can use one for all the different phases and aspects of your life purpose:
- to help you brainstorm and create
- to plan the logistics
- to gather information with which to make better choices and decisions

Flow Charts

Mind maps are great for creative and nonlinear planning, but sometimes you just want to get from here to there in the fastest and most efficient manner. In this case, a straight line is called for. Of all the tools available to you, a flow chart is one of the most popular tools for plotting a direct path.

There are two ways to create a flow chart:
1. Start where you are now and chart the steps to get to your destination.
2. Start at your destination and work backward to where you are now.

Flow charts can flow in any direction that works for you — from top to bottom, bottom to top, right to left, or from left to right. Use whichever direction makes more sense to you.

Creating a flow chart is quite simple, even though you can certainly make it complicated and complex, if you wish. It can even begin to look a bit like a mind map. The difference between a flow chart and a mind map is that the mind map works from the center outward in all directions. The flow chart works in a linear mode from one direction to another.

If you're comfortable with computer programs, there is flow chart software available to help with the organization of it. For some people this works great. Others, however, get lost in trying to learn the software and never get to the point of actually creating a chart. If you're one of these folks, it might be best for you to get a large piece of paper and do it by hand, using the tools you already have from creating your mind map.

To experience the effectiveness of a flow chart, select something from the mind map you created earlier — something you want to achieve or attain. Use a large sheet of paper such as the type you used for your mind map to create your flow chart.

Before you begin, decide if you're starting at the beginning or if you want to work backwards from the end result. Then determine *where* on the paper you'll place the beginning and the end result. If your steps seem to come to you in a less than linear form, don't fret. Simply plug them in where they seem most appropriate for now. You can adjust them later, as you work with your chart.

The Timeline Chart

"Omigod! Where am I going to find all the time I need for this?"

"There's so much to do... I don't know what to do first."

"How can I fit all this into my schedule?"

Sound familiar? Have you heard some of these qualms in your head?

Never fear, for there's a handy tool for organizing your time — one that can be used in conjunction with your mind maps and your flow charts. It's called a timeline chart.

The timeline chart is a great tool for visualizing your available time and planning how you'll use it. Whenever you foresee an issue of time usage, this chart is an excellent tool to help you gain clarity of what needs to be done and when. You can use it for your entire life purpose journey, or for any portion of it. The timeline chart helps you identify the chunks of time you'll need for each of the tasks within any project so that you can easily visualize how you're filling up your time. Any overlaps in scheduling will instantly become apparent so that you can correct them *before* you find yourself trying to run in two different directions at the same time.

Timeline charts are actually quite simple to set up, using a columnar pad or paper on which rows and columns have been drawn. They're created in three basic steps:

1. In the far lest column, list all the things you want to accomplish within a certain time frame, such as a week, a month or a year.
2. In the top row, moving from left to right, in each column indicate the sequential chunks of time you want to use, such as hours, days, weeks or months. You can use typical calendar periods (July, August, September) or number the time frames (week 12, week 13).
3. Estimate how much time you'll need for each item you listed in the left column and draw a horizontal line designating that time, from start to time of completion.

You can use colors to indicate different people, contractors, or businesses who may be the ones doing the various parts of your project. Many items may be happening simultaneously, and the timeline chart will allow you to see if the work is being handled in a balanced manner or if the heaviest part of the workload is falling on one person or business. With the timeline chart, you'll be able to track how the items are flowing sequentially and notice any areas where not enough or too much time is being allowed.

You may want to do several timeline charts for your life purpose, beginning with one big chart for the overall project, then create others that divide that chart into additional charts with smaller time increments. For example, if you have a five year plan, you may also want to have timeline charts for each year or each six month period.

Important or Urgent or Both or Neither?

As you begin creating your plans, it's inevitable that you'll run into planning conflicts. When you create a timeline chart, for example, you may find that everything is in one time period. There will be other occasions, too, when you'll find yourself with multiple items you wish to accomplish — all within the same time frame. Or you may find the things you want to do piling up until you feel overwhelmed.

Prioritizing what you choose to do and when you choose to do it will make your life purpose journey much smoother. Everything you do can be prioritized into one of these four levels:

- Urgent and important
- Urgent but not important
- Important but not urgent
- Not urgent and not important

Before you begin to prioritize, it's very important to define what the two words "urgent" and "important" mean to you in relation to the things you want to accomplish.

The definitions may change depending upon the project you're prioritizing and where you are in the progress of the project. For example, one of my clients wanted to teach a class in two months time. She defined "urgent" as the items that needed to be complete within three days of the class. To her, "important" meant it had to be done anytime before the class. Had she chosen a more distant date for her class, her definitions would have been different. A date closer to the present might have put everything in the "urgent" category.

Select a project from your mind map that you'd like to prioritize. With that project in mind, write your definition of these two words:

Important:

Urgent

The definitions of these two words will change depending upon the circumstances. Each time you use this prioritization tool, remember to first define what these words mean to you in relation to the items or project you're prioritizing.

Now, using the items that you want to prioritize, insert them in the most appropriate categories.

Important and Urgent

Urgent but not Important

Important but not Urgent

Not Important and Not Urgent

Is everything you have on your list in the "Important and Urgent" square? If so, identify the items that could be moved to a less urgent or less important rating, and move them. If you find that you really can't move anything out of the "Important and Urgent" square, go back to your definitions and redefine them. Then see what items you can move out of the "Important and Urgent" square.

Play with this for a while, moving your items into more appropriate categories, until you feel comfortable with the prioritization you've assigned each item and with the balance of quantities in each category.

Use this prioritization tool when you:
- begin to feel overwhelmed
- think that you're trying to juggle too much
- don't have enough time to get everything done

Goal Setting Tools

Your main goal of living your life purpose may be quite a monumental leap from where you're standing right now. Attempting to get from here to there in one giant step can be quite a daunting challenge. You can lessen your chances of becoming overwhelmed and increase your chances of success by setting interim goals.

The steps you have on your flow chart are interim goals — smaller steps on the way to the larger, main goal of living your life purpose. When you break your main goal into smaller, bite-sized chunks you're giving yourself goals that are much easier to accomplish. As you complete these smaller, interim goals, you'll be motivated with a sense of accomplishment that will support and uplift you on the way to realizing your main goal.

Years ago, a client asked me for assistance in completing her goal of building a website and getting it online. She had taken a website design class from me several years previously, and had not progressed from the preliminary planning stages in the design of her website. During one of our first coaching sessions, when I asked her what was next, she replied, "Oh, I guess I'll just continue on as I have been." Whoa Nelly! No wonder she wasn't moving ahead. She was stuck in the nowhereland between the start and the end of her goal with no interim goals in between. All she had was the beginning and the end. We discussed interim goals, achievements, and accomplishments, and within a week she began to move forward. Within three months she completed her website and had it online!

You, too, need interim goals to use as stepping stones, road marks, and mile posts in order to move incrementally forward toward your main goals.

Guidelines for Successful Goal Setting

Before you begin to create your goals, consider these guidelines to better ensure your success:

> **1. Make sure your goals are specific and measurable.** How will you know you're done racing if you have no finish line? How will you know you've accomplished your goal if you have no way of recognizing it? Consider measurability both in time and quantity.
> **2. Make your goals achievable.** There is nothing more discouraging than setting a goal that's too big and then not being able to achieve it. Make it a bit of a stretch so that it's challenging, but not so huge that you'll become disheartened and discouraged because it's simply too big or too much for you to attain.

3. Make it your goal. You cannot set goals for other people and expect any measure of success. They'll resent you *and* the goals, and will put all their energy into resistance. Nor can others set goals for you. A goal inflicted upon you by someone else is a goal that will never be accomplished. Worse, it robs you of energy as you resent and resist the imposition. Also, don't set goals in which the result depends upon someone else. This makes the goal someone else's.

4. Consider the ecological aspects of your goal. How will accomplishing this goal affect others in your life, such as your family, co-workers, clients, and friends? These people are also stakeholders in the outcome of your goals and how your goals affect them will influence whether they support or resist you.

From the steps on your flow chart, list five interim goals that you intend to achieve.

1.

2.

3.

4.

5.

Review these goals and check each one to make sure that they conform to the four guidelines for successful goal setting:

- What is the measurement by which you'll know when you've achieved this goal?
- Can you realistically achieve this goal?
- Was this goal your idea or someone else's?
- Who are the stakeholders involved in each of your goals? Note their name(s) next to the particular goal in which they have an interest in the outcome. How might these people affect the outcome of the goal? How might they affect you — your energy, attitude, and emotions — as you work toward attaining the goal? This very important issue will be addressed in more depth during Chapter 7.

Lists and Notes

Right now you may be thinking, "I'm already very familiar with making lists. Everyone does lists. What's the big deal about making lists?" Grocery lists, to-do lists, guest lists… they're all a part of your daily life and are invaluable as reminders. However, lists serve a role much more important than simply reminding you to buy milk and pick up the drycleaning.

Lists help to bring your thoughts out of the invisible world of your mind and into the physical world so you can work with them. One of the first steps of manifesting your goals is to get them out of your head, where they reside as energy in the form of an idea or thought, and into the physical world as a written plan, goal, or list.

Lists can relieve or even eliminate the sense of being overwhelmed with stuff to do. There will be times when you just can't avoid feeling overwhelmed by all the things running around in your head as you begin to create the plan for living your life purpose. Writing them on a list gets them out of your head and onto paper so that you can see just exactly how much you have to do. Generally, you'll find that the quantity of your list is much less than you thought when it was racing around inside your brain.

Lists also serve as a vital part of manifesting a bigger plan. They're some of the stepping stones you create on the journey toward your goal of living your life purpose. They help you to divide the bigger goal into many smaller goals that are easier to accomplish.

Lists are great motivational tools. They make it easy to visualize the progress you've made as you check off the items you've accomplished. The satisfaction you receive as you cross off an item is a great way to reward yourself for doing the work. As you complete an item on your list and cross it off, the feeling of satisfaction you get is a fabulous motivator that will keep you moving forward toward your goal.

Lists can also be used as an aid in planning your next steps. Your mind map, flow chart, and timeline chart all give you an overall viewpoint but may not contain much detail. Creating lists as you go along will help you divide the bigger steps into smaller steps, which will help to keep you moving forward every day toward fully living your life purpose.

Lists and flow charts have some similarities. Both include things you want to do and goals you intend to accomplish. However, lists are a visual array of things, while flow charts are sequential.

Lists serve the purpose of being reminders of the myriad chores, tasks, and necessities of life. They, and mind maps, are much like a tossed salad — all the ingredients are there but they're not organized, measured, or sequential. Flow charts and timeline charts are more like cake recipes — measured ingredients combined in a logical and sequential method.

Sometimes while you're in the midst of making of a list, inspiration will attack and a new list will be born. For instance, while making a list of intended accomplishments for the upcoming year, I was inspired to create another list of the classes I'd love to teach during the year. That list inspired me to list the content of the classes, which I then used as an outline for creating the classes.

Here are some ways you can use lists:

1. Make a list at the end of each day of things you want to accomplish the next day.
2. Make a weekly list of things you want to accomplish.
3. Share your list with your mate, your kids, a friend, or a co-worker and ask them to review it with you at the end of the day. This is a powerful method for gaining support.
4. Use sticky notes to write down your action steps and place them in strategic places, such as on your bathroom mirror and on the inside of your front door.
5. Insert your to-do list in your "Tasks" on your PDA.
6. Download your to-do list onto your computer.
7. Set the alarm on your PDA or your computer program to remind you of the important things on your to-do list.
8. Send an email to yourself at the end of the day with your to-do list for the next day.

Planning Through the Chakras

Just in the off chance you haven't ever heard of chakras, they're energy centers or vortexes that reside within your physical body. Even if you aren't familiar with chakras, you've probably experienced their energy. When you feel a sense of love emanating from your heart, you're feeling the energy of the fourth chakra — the heart chakra — as it expands. When you feel like someone has knocked the wind out of you by violating one of your personal boundaries, you're feeling a direct hit to your third chakra, or "will center".

There are seven main chakras in your body, with additional chakras both inside and outside your body. Those chakras that are outside your body are in your other energy fields, or bodies, such as your aura. This section deals with only the seven major chakras that reside within your physical body.

These seven chakras are vertically aligned in the center of your body, from the top of your head to the base of your torso, and point outward on a horizontal plane. The energy of each of the chakras vibrates at different rates of speed with the slowest vibration being the root chakra and the fastest vibration being the crown chakra. The chakras are identified either by name or number, with the numbers beginning at the root chakra.

> **The First Chakra:**
> Named the "root chakra" it's located in your pelvic area and is associated with the physical world
> **The Second Chakra:**
> Named the "sacral chakra", it's located in your lower abdomen and is associated with the creative force, family, friends, and community.

The Third Chakra:
Named the "will center", it's located in your solar plexus and is associated with generating and focusing personal energy or drive.

The Fourth Chakra:
Named the "heart chakra", it's located in the area of your heart and is associated with the feeling of love.

The Fifth Chakra:
Named the "throat chakra", it's located in the center of your throat and is associated with creativity and transformation of thought and vision into words.

The Sixth Chakra:
Named the "third eye", it's located between your eyebrows and above them about an inch. It's associated with inner vision.

The Seventh Chakra:
Named the "crown chakra", it's located at the top, or crown, of your head and is where you receive inspiration from your guides, angels, Higher Self, and other divine sources of higher wisdom.

From inspiration to manifestation, each of the chakras are steps used when creating. Using the chakras, the process of creation begins at the crown chakra and flows as follows:

- **Your crown chakra** is where you receive the inspiration for your plan or project.
- **Your third eye** is where you receive the visual form of your inspiration and "see" it with your inner vision.
- **Your throat chakra** is where you transform thought and vision into words. This is the first manifestation on the physical plane of the inspiration you received through your crown chakra.

- **Your heart chakra** is where you feel the love and passion for your inspiration, giving you the desire to proceed toward physically creating it.
- **Your center of will chakra** is where you generate and focus the force of your energy, or drive, as you move into action.
- **Your sacral chakra** is where you share your inspiration with other people.
- **Your root chakra** is the pathway for birthing your inspiration into the physical world.

Let's use the example of writing a book using the process of creation through the chakras.

- The inspiration for the book is received through your **crown chakra**. You experience it as a great idea that just seemed to come to you.
- With the inner vision of your **third eye**, you see what you want to write about. You may visualize the interaction of the people in your book, how they look, and what their surroundings are like.
- You then begin to transform the vision of your book into writing with your **throat chakra**, as your inspiration begins to solidify into the concepts and messages you want to share with your writing.
- The love and passion you feel in your **heart chakra** for the inspiration of your book gives you the desire to write it.
- With the power of your **will chakra** you move into action, as you put words to paper, research publishers and editors, and draw your design for the book cover.
- Through the energy of your **sacral chakra** you gather other people to help you manifest your book, such as editors, publishers, printers, and book designers.

- At last you manifest your reality by using the energy of the **root chakra** and your book is published!

Creating Through Your Chakras

In the following exercise you might use your life purpose plan in its entirety, or perhaps you might want to use just one part of it. Starting at your seventh chakra, the chakra of divine inspiration, write your thoughts about each level and how it relates to your life purpose. As you do so, you'll be creating an energetic pathway from your initial inspiration to actual physical reality.

Seventh Chakra – Crown: Your inspirations, thoughts, and ideas

Sixth Chakra – Third Eye: The images and pictures you have about your life purpose with your inner vision

Fifth Chakra – Throat: The words you use, written or spoken, as you transform your creative vision into communication

Fourth Chakra – Heart: The passion and love you feel for your purposeful work

Third Chakra – Will: Transforming your words and passion into action

Second Chakra – Sacral: The other members of your creative family and what parts they play

First Chakra – Root: The manifestation into physical reality

Feel free to play with this and use it however it best suits you. You can begin at any one of the chakras to which you feel drawn. For example, you may have a huge passion, a burning desire, a raging love for a certain type of work; you might start at the fourth chakra, the heart chakra, and work in either direction. If you want to understand the higher aspects of the work you're already doing, use this process in reverse, starting at the first chakra and working up through all the chakras to the seventh.

All of the exercises in this book are meant to assist you in gaining deeper insights and in widening your range of perspectives. You can change the rules of any of these exercises to make them more valuable to you as learning tools and tools of creation to use on your journey to living your life purpose.

Notes:

Success

The definition of success according to most dictionaries is:
"The attainment of wealth, favor, or eminence."

That's *their* definition. However, the most important definition of success is *yours*.

You can have all the money, fame, and expensive toys in the world and still feel like a failure. If you don't *feel* successful in your heart and soul, then despite what any authorities on the meaning of words say, you're *not* successful.

True success resides in your heart. You *know* when you have success because of how you feel, not how big the number is in your bank account or how many islands you own. We've all heard stories of fabulously wealthy people who, despite the enormous amount of their acquisitions, still feel unsatisfied with their lives. What they lack isn't more money… it's the soul deep satisfaction of living their life purpose.

In a recent poll of top-level executives, more than 90% of them said they felt like frauds and that the work they were doing wasn't worth the great sums of money they were being paid. Why would they feel that way? Because in truth they're living a life that's based on fraud — they're living someone else's life. They aren't being true to themselves and their own path. They're defining themselves and the success of their work using someone else's definition. Had they been living their own definition of success, they would now be experiencing the fabulous success that truly counts — that of living *their* life purpose.

Take inventory of the people you know or know of. How many of them would you deem to be successful? Write the names of five people you consider to be highly successful here:

1.
2.
3.
4.
5.

Of these five people, circle the names of those who you believe to be following their hearts and passionately living their life purpose.

How would you like to be among that group?

What *is* Success?

Boy howdy, isn't that the question of the century? Not too long ago, back in the '80s and '90s, there was no question about the meaning of success. One's lifestyle was the proof of it. The more wealth a person displayed, the more successful they were deemed to be.

Remember the saying from an era now passed, "Whoever dies

with the most toys wins"? Many people found this to be very humorous. After the laughter faded away, however, many people realized the cosmic joke — we still died. And we can't take our toys with us.

Today, many people are still judging their lives and the lives of others by the size of their house, the price of their cars, where and how they vacation, and how many expensive toys they have. By now you're no doubt questioning that bygone standard and are wondering, "so if we don't define success by the dollar amount, how *do* we define it?"

The trick answer to that question is that *we* don't define success. *You* define success.

What may mean success for one person may look like failure to another. Donald Trump may be the epitome of success for many because of his monumental financial wealth; but for just as many others he may be the epitome of failure because he focuses on acquisition of financial wealth and not spiritual wealth. Some believe those who join the Peace Corp are losers who can't find real jobs. Yet others hold the belief that these volunteers, who have the courage to follow their hearts, live highly successful lives.

This is an opportune time for a gentle reminder: your definition of success is much like your boundaries. It's about *you* and what's important to you. It's for you to own, and not to be used as a standard by which to judge other people and how they choose to live their lives. You have a unique life purpose with unique life experiences that you've set up for yourself... as have others. Honor them as they traverse their path, and respect them for the work they've set up for themselves, as you honor and respect yourself as you traverse your own life path. The bottom line is that *you* define success for *you*.

As Albert Schweitzer said:

"Success is not the key to happiness. Happiness is the key to success. If you love what you are doing, you will be successful."

What's So Important About Success?

Success is another major clue that will guide you to your path of living your life purpose. Each time you feel success about an accomplishment, it's an indication that you're moving in the right direction.

It isn't only the achieving of success that's important. What you gain as you journey on your path to mastery is important. Along the way you will learn such things as:

Trust
- Trusting yourself
- Trusting your inner wisdom
- Trusting that others wish to help you
- Trusting that others love you
- Trusting that we are all in this game together

Confidence
- Confidence that *you can* do it
- Confidence that you are not alone
- Confidence that you have unlimited access to assistance in unlimited forms
- Confidence in your own abilities
- Confidence in your own inner strength

Faith

- Faith that the Universe/God/Goddess/Spirit is on your side
- Faith that you have unlimited support from your guides, angels, the Universe, your higher self, and a multitude of other spiritual sources
- Faith that your spiritual resources are *always* available for support
- Faith in your own abilities
- Faith in the value of your life purpose
- Faith that what you are doing truly is of value to others

Mastery: Another Word for Success

Achieving mastery of anything is a grand success. No matter how large or small, how simple or complex, there are opportunities for achieving mastery in everything you do.

The path of mastery is measured in four levels, beginning with unconscious incompetence and ending in mastery:

> **Unconscious incompetence:** This the level where you don't know that you don't know. At this point you're oblivious about what you must know in order to achieve the success you desire.

> **Conscious incompetence:** When you arrive at this stage of mastery, you realize that you don't know what you need to know, and begin your search to find out what it is.

> **Conscious competence:** At this stage, you've learned the mechanics of what you need to know, but are still becoming comfortable with your new knowledge.

Unconscious competence: At last — Mastery! Success! Now you know what you need to know. In fact, you know it so well that you don't have to think about how you do it.

Learning to drive a car demonstrates how this principle works.

Unconscious Incompetence: You don't know that you don't know how to drive a car (this would probably be when you're an infant!).

Conscious Incompetence: When you're near the age where your older siblings and maybe some school chums are driving, you realize that you don't yet know how to drive and decide to learn.

Conscious Competence: As you begin to learn about driving, and all that it entails, you realize how much there is to learn and how much more you have to learn before you earn your driver's license. All those pedals and levers and things! Not to mention all the rules and laws.

Unconscious Competence: Years after becoming a licensed driver, you buzz down the freeway, casually listening to your favorite music as you adeptly maneuver in the traffic. Driving has become so automatic that you don't even think about how you do it. *This* is the state of mastery.

There are many things in which you've achieved mastery during your life. Reading, for one. Mastering the ability to read is quite an accomplishment. Just ask anyone who is currently struggling to learn a language that's foreign to them.

In the space below, list at least five things in which you've begun at the stage of unconscious incompetence and have gone on to successfully achieve mastery.

1.

2.

3.

4.

5.

Keep this list handy, and when you begin to doubt your capability to achieve success, refer to it.

The Importance of Defining Success for Yourself

Success is a very important marker along your path of progress, commonly called "life". You're programmed to move away from things that don't feel good to you — things like failure and defeat. You move towards things that feel good, such as... you guessed it... success! So when you have a small success as you move toward a larger goal, it's a marker or a sign telling you that you're moving in the right direction.

Experiences which you may consider failures are actually very valuable as indicators showing you the need for some course corrections to get moving again in the right direction toward success. We'll work more with so-called failures later.

As you travel along your path you'll have many successes. Some you may consider to be larger and more important than others, but they're *all* successes. They *all* serve to help you stay on course toward living your life purpose as you journey through this lifetime.

How to Know When You're Successful

If you don't know what success looks like for you, or how you feel when you're successful, how can you possibly know when you have it? Without a clear definition of success you could lose your direction and wander around in circles, or worse, end up going in direction that leads you away from living your life purpose.

Knowing how you feel when you experience success is necessary for attracting what you want and manifesting it. You'll be using that feeling in some of the exercises in the next chapter on motivation and manifesting.

How do you know when you're successful? The answer to this question lies in first of all defining what success means to you.

Sometimes it's quite simple to know when you're successful. If you want to hit a home run during a baseball game, and you do it, you're successful. But success isn't always as easy to recognize. Sometimes it's nebulous and ethereal. Sometimes it's not recognized until some time after the fact. And sometimes it's not recognized at all.

In this chapter, you're going to wallow in success until you know it inside and out. When you've reached the end of this chapter there should be no doubt in your mind how you define success and how it feels to you.

Remembering Your Successes

Everyone has had successes in their life. No matter how young or old you are, what your station is in life, or what you've experienced during your time on this planet, you've had successes. They may be so small, or so big, that you couldn't see them as such, but you did have successes.

Think back over your life and bring back memories you have of past successes. As they come back to you, briefly describe a few of them in the space below:

1.

2.

3.

4.

5.

From *your* perspective, what defined each of these as successes?

What is the common theme that connects them?

Were you doing what you loved?

Did you overcome great adversity to achieve this success?

Which of your life values are represented?

Success and Your Life Values

As you may have noticed, the subject of life values comes up a lot in these exercises. Your life values continue to be of paramount importance throughout this book, as they are throughout your life.

You'll see the question "Which of your life values are reflected in this?" being presented to you again and again. Sometimes it may be phrased in the reverse, such as "Which of your life values are *not* represented here?" As you complete the exercises and reflect on which of your life values are or are not included, you'll discover how vitally important your life values are in living your life purpose. If you aren't living in alignment with your values, you aren't living your life purpose with any success. You may be living it partially, or you may even be living someone else's, but unless you're totally in alignment with *your* life values you aren't a success at living your own life purpose.

Throughout this book you'll have plenty of opportunity to integrate your life values into your daily routine, until it becomes second nature for you to consciously filter everything you think and do through them.

Your Grande Success

Go back through the successes you described in the previous exercise and select one that was particularly important for you. Describe it more completely here, getting as detailed as you possibly can. Begin by noting your intent or goal, if you had one, as you started on your path of achieving your success.

How clear were you about what you intended to achieve when you began?

At what point did you know that you were successful?

How did you feel emotionally when you knew you had achieved this success?

What did you feel physically as you experienced this success? What sensations did you notice in your body? Where in your body did you feel then?

At this point a clearer picture of what success means to you should be appearing. For the purpose of becoming even more clear, repeat this exercise for each of the successes you listed in the previous exercise.

Failure: The Other Side of Success

Failure has been described as the other side of the hand called "Success". However, what you think of as failure is actually another step on the way to success. Failure is an opportunity to learn more about living your life purpose, or more appropriately, how you *don't* want to live it. Each failure offers the opportunity to learn more about what isn't a part of your life purpose, so that you know without a shred of doubt what *is* a part of it.

All of the people who you think are successes have an intimate knowledge of failure. They know that failure is simply another step in the process that gets them to success. Thomas Edison, when he was inventing the light bulb, is quoted as saying, "I have not failed. I have just found 10,000 ways that won't work." Henry Ford said, "Failure is only the opportunity to more intelligently begin again." If either of these men had quit after the first few unsuccessful attempts, we would have been deprived of their wonderful inventions.

Failure isn't failure unless you quit. As long as you don't give up, you're still moving along your path toward success. The following story illustrates this point.

The view from my office is my back yard. Since it abuts a greenbelt, I've left most of it in its natural state. There's a wonderful variety of wildlife that passes by my office window every day — deer, raccoons, chipmunks, and all kinds of birds. Both the birds and the chipmunks are drawn to the seed in the birdfeeder right outside my office window.

This birdfeeder has a "squirrel proof" shield on it and is hung quite high on a metal pole. However, this contraption apparently isn't "chipmunk proof." Recently I was entertained by a very determined chipmunk who spent days figuring out how to leap just so from the pole to the birdfeeder. It would carefully eyeball the situation, gauging how much oomph to put in its leap and where to aim for the best landing. It fell many times and, after a moment or two, would immediately scamper back up the pole to try again, using the information from its most recent attempt to improve its aerial acrobatics.

It soon became so adept at aiming its jump that it was no longer missing the feeder. It would scamper up the pole to the exact spot it knew was the best launching place, leap with the exact amount of push-off, and land exactly where it knew it could easily grab toe-holds.

This chipmunk is one very smart, and now very fat, little critter. It proved without a doubt that...

Failure isn't failure. It's learning.

Each time you experience a setback in achieving one of your goals, you're gaining knowledge that will assist you not only as you work toward your goal but also will make the end result far better. You'll find valuable information lurking in that so-called "failure", guaranteed.

Your Most Grande Failure

No doubt you have had experiences in your life which you labeled as failure. In this exercise you'll have the opportunity to take a fresh look at one of your "failures" and see it from a different perspective.

Think of a time when, in your eyes, you failed. Describe it completely, getting as detailed as you can. Use additional paper if you need to.

What did you learn from this experience? List at least five things.

1.

2.

3.

4.

5.

How did learning these things help you at a later time?

1.

2.

3.

4.

5.

What are the gifts this failure gave you? How did it contribute to making you the wonderful person you are today?

What are the successes that you now see in this experience?

How are your life values are reflected in this experience?

The Qualities of Success

Success has many qualities which can make it difficult to describe succinctly, easily, and completely. Sometimes it's easier to recognize success when it appears outside of yourself, such as when you see it in another person.

Who do you view as successful? List up to five people whom you admire and consider to be successful. After their names list the qualities that, in your opinion, make them successful.

1.

2.

3.

4.

5.

Which of these qualities do you have?

Which of these qualities would you like to have more of?

How do these qualities relate to your life values? (There are those life values, *again!*)

Your Fans Want to Know...

Imagine that you're fully living your life purpose. You've already achieved the grandest of success and you're acknowledged and respected by many for your work. One of your admirers writes you a letter to ask how you became so successful. Write your answer here:

Dear _____,

Gratefully yours,

What little gems did you discover about your success in this letter?

A Letter to Yourself: Part 1

You already have the knowledge and wisdom to easily achieve success and live your life purpose. It's just hidden within you somewhere. One of the ways to access some of that treasure of knowledge is by using a very simple technique — writing a letter to yourself. As you write the letter, you automatically engage your imagination to access the creative portion of your brain. Your results may astound you!

For this exercise, imagine that you're 90 years old and have long since attained the level of success you only dreamed about when you were much younger (the age you are now). Write a letter to your younger self, sharing any wisdom you've gained through your years of experience that you think might help this younger person attain the success they so much desire.

Dear _____,

Lovingly Yours,

Take a few moments to come back to the present time, and then read what you just wrote. Highlight or underline any nuggets of wisdom your older and wiser self shared with you.

Which of your life values are reflected in these gems of wisdom?

A Letter to Yourself: Part 2

Within the innocence of children lie untold amounts of wealth in the form of wisdom and knowledge. You can access the wisdom of your inner child by writing a letter.

Close your eyes, and imagine that you're five years old. You might also imagine that you're very precocious and already know how to read and write! Now, as this wise five-year-old, begin writing your letter. Share with the older you what you believe is important in the attainment of success.

Dear _____,

Love,

After you've written this letter, read it over. What wisdom did your inner child have for you?

Revisit these letters often for inspiration, encouragement, and maybe a giggle or two.

Wallowing in the Success of Living Your Life Purpose

Ahhhh, the feeling of success. There's nothing like it.

Emotions and physical sensations are two of the main communication methods between you and your sources of higher wisdom. The feelings you have are major guideposts, keeping you on the path of living your life purpose. Pleasant, satisfying sensations guide you toward the elements of your life purpose, while feelings that don't feel so good tend to drive you away from anything that isn't in alignment with it.

The *feeling* of success is one of the strongest of the guideposts that brings you closer to living your life purpose.

To gain maximum clarity about how success feels as you live your life purpose, complete these sentences using the appropriate emotional or physical feelings — or both. If you have difficulty coming up with examples, use your imagination and pretend that you're already doing something you plan to do at a later date. You may have several different emotions *and* physical feelings when you experience success. Complete one sentence for each of the feelings you have, using additional paper if needed:

I'm integrating the essence of my life purpose into my life by
_____and as I succeed, I feel

_____.

I'm integrating the essence of my life purpose into my life by
_____and as I succeed, I feel

_____.

I'm integrating the essence of my life purpose into my life by _____and as I succeed, I feel

_____.

I'm integrating the essence of my life purpose into my life by
_____and as I succeed, I feel

_____.

I'm integrating the essence of my life purpose into my life by
_____and as I succeed, I feel

_____.

Review what you've just written. What are the patterns or repeated themes in the feelings you have when you feel successful?

Which of your life values are reflected in your feelings of success?

As stated at the beginning of this chapter, knowing what success means to you is important because… well, how will you know you have it if you don't know what it is? A successful life is one lived in alignment with your life purpose. A huge part of achieving this goal of success is in knowing when you're moving closer to it *and* in knowing when you actually *are* living it.

Every time you recognize a success and take the time to celebrate it, you're inserting a marker in your life — a milestone in your progress toward living your life purpose.

When you're *absolutely clear* about how you feel when you have achieved success, no matter how small or large it may seem, you're growing the feeling of success that's stored in the emotional memory of your brain. Each time you add another success to your emotional memory, you make it easier for your brain to recall this feeling of success. It then becomes easier for you to create successes because you can easily recognize when you're having a success and can identify exactly what defines the success. You become more adept at recognizing the elements of your success and it becomes easier for you to create more successes for yourself. It's a wonderful upward spiral! The more you feel success, the more you want to feel it, and the more you *can* feel it.

In addition, it's very important to be able to recognize how success feels to you in order to facilitate the visioning work you'll be doing later. You'll be enhancing your vision work with the addition of certain feelings and emotions, which makes the results more powerful. The feeling of success is one of the most important pieces that you'll use for this work. You'll be able to reach your goals more quickly and have grander successes when you can use the feeling you get when you've achieved a success in your goal setting and vision work.

Notes

Motivation and Manifesting

Motivation and manifesting work hand in hand with each other. Understanding what motivates you (why you want something) adds power and speed to your manifesting and increases your ability to obtain what you want. Both are very useful tools to have with you as you journey toward living your life purpose.

In this chapter you'll identify your motivators you and how best to use them to your advantage.

You'll also learn what you've been doing and continue to do that creates what's in front of you now — your home, your work, the state of your finances, the quality of people in your life, and more. You'll discover tools to help you consciously manifest what you want.

You'll combine the use of your motivators *and* knowledge of manifesting to help you move more directly and with more speed toward successfully living your life purpose.

Like most people, you may not be consciously aware of how you create the things and events in your life. So first, let's find out what moves you into action (your motivators) and then hone your manifesting skills.

What Are Motivators?

People are motivated by a variety of things, but what motivates you may have no effect or may even have the opposite effect on someone else. As an example, fear can be a great motivator, or it can have the opposite effect by stopping forward movement. Fear can stir you to action or it can create an extreme state of non-movement that may even develop into a catatonic state. Same thing, different effects. When you understand what motivates you, you can use it *consciously* to get you moving toward what you want — successfully living your life purpose.

Many times while traveling the path of your life purpose you'll get bogged down or stuck. We'll deal more with what stops you and what to do when this happens in Chapter 9. For now, the focus is on what gets you moving. Using your motivators *consciously* will get you unstuck and propel you out of the muck and mire of "stuckdom" and back onto your path, moving forward to create the life you desire.

The things that motivate you are values, and although they typically aren't your life values, some of these motivating values may show up in that department. These particular values are called attracting values and repelling values. Their name describes what they do: they either pull you toward a thing or move you away from it.

The donkey driver who takes no chances with a stubborn donkey and uses both a carrot and a stick is a perfect example of attracting and repelling values. The carrot is dangled in front of the donkey, which the donkey moves toward, and the stick is used on its behind, which the donkey moves away from.

Likewise, you have carrots and sticks that will assist you in moving yourself in the direction you wish to go — values that move you toward something and values that move you away from something. The motivating values that are attracting you toward what you desire are your carrots, and your sticks are those values that repel you away from what you don't desire.

When you know what those motivating values are, you can use them as powerful tools on your journey toward living your life purpose. Not only will they come in handy when you find yourself stuck and unable to move forward, but you'll be able to use them *before* you find yourself stopped. Using the plan you created for living your life purpose, you can associate the appropriate motivators with important steps *before* taking action to add horsepower to your forward movement.

My own discovery that fear is one of my most powerful motivators may serve as an example of how these things work. I had a well-paying job as a construction project superintendent, so I bought a house and a new truck. Life was wonderful, until one day the owner of the company had a mental breakdown and closed the company. One day I had a good job, and the next day I was without any income except unemployment insurance. There were no well-paying jobs within 100 miles of where I lived. After much mental deliberation, I decided to talk with the real estate agent who sold me my house to ask about becoming a real estate agent.

Six months later I was one, but still had no income except for unemployment, which barely paid the bills. Fear of not being able to make my house payment and my other bills motivated me to work harder than anyone else in that office. I had a sign next to my phone which read:

There's only one way to overcome fear.
Go out and scare yourself.

And that's exactly what I did. Every day I did something that scared me — knocking on the door of a home for sale by the owner, visiting a construction site and talking to the builder about listing his house with me, calling people I didn't know to ask them about using me as their real estate agent. I used my fear of not being able to keep a roof over my head to drive me forward in my work.

Within six months in my new career as a realtor, I was receiving enough in commissions to feel a bit more comfortable; within a year I was earning the same as I had been in my construction job. Within two years I was one of the top producers in our office, and by the third year I was making three times the money that I had been getting in my position as project superintendent.

Using my repelling value of fear to motivate me forward toward financial success worked very well.

What Motivates You?

When you know what both your attracting and repelling motivators are, you have a powerful tool kit to use every day to propel you toward living your life purpose.

Before you can use your motivating values, however, you must know what they are.

Here is a partial list of some typical examples of motivating values, both attracting and repelling values:

Love	Fear	Guilt	Poverty
Dare	Competition	Wealth	Shame
Security	Praise	Rewards	Health
Scolding	Revenge	Learning	Winning
Deadlines	Achievement	Fun	Rejection
Challenge	Losing	Acceptance	Money
Pain	Fame	Nagging	Responsibility
	Control	Acknowledgment	

List five values that motivate you in the space below. You can use the values above and also insert others that work for you. If any of your life values are appropriate as motivating values, use them too.

1.
2.
3.
4.
5.

If you experience difficulty in identifying your motivators, think back to a time when you had a task or a project to complete and found yourself at a standstill, solidly stuck in the Lack of Motivation Bog. What was it that eventually got you moving?

Which Way Do You Want to Go?

Although motivation comes in many forms, all motivators fall into one of two categories: attracting or repelling, the carrot or the stick.

Go back through the motivating values that you listed previously and separate them into two lists — one which includes your repelling values and one with your attracting values.

Attracting Motivators	Repelling Motivators
1.	1.
2.	2.
3.	3.
4.	4.
5.	5.

Motivating Values in Your Past

You've used these motivating values all your life and probably haven't been aware of how you've used them... or even that you've used them at all. In order to understand how you use your motivating values, think back to a time when you desired something and obtained it — a car, a new place to live, a different job, a toy, etc.

Describe what you did to acquire it. Begin with what you wanted and why you wanted it.

What were the motivating values that propelled you into action?

Were they attracting values, repelling values, or some of each?

Were there other motivating values involved that aren't currently on your list? If so, note them here and also add them to your list in either the attracting or the repelling values category.

Using Your Motivating Values Today

Describe a situation in which you're currently having difficulty moving toward your goal.

Which of your attracting values might you use to pull you toward your goal?

Which of your repelling values might you use to propel you toward it?

What actions will you take to use these motivators to assist you to get moving in the direction you want? List at least five action steps you can take using your attracting and repelling values.

Moving Toward

1.

2.

3.

4.

5.

Moving Away From

1.

2.

3.

4.

5.

Motivating Values and Life Values

You knew this was coming, didn't you? Keep in mind that your life values are connected to everything you think, do, and feel. Everything you do in this workbook — and in your life — is related to your life values. As you become more aware of how they permeate everything, you'll be able to use them more easily to make conscious choices that allow your life to flow more smoothly.

The alignment of your life values and your motivating values is important in this regard. For your motivating values to work most effectively, they need to be in alignment with your life values.

Remember that the most effortless way to live your life is from the inside out, using your life values as the filters to test whether a choice or an action is in alignment with your life purpose. It's impossible to do your life purpose work without also honoring your life values. This would be a contradiction of spiritual law.

If you use motivators that are in conflict with your values, you'll be caught in the dyadic energy created by this conflict and won't be able to move forward. Instead, you'll be constantly bouncing back and forth between your motivators and your life values, like a ping-pong ball in play.

As an example, imagine you're on a basketball team. If one of your life values is community and you're using a motivating value of fame, a conflict might arise within you when someone on your team begins to out-perform you and gets all the attention and acknowledgment from the coach, the supporters, and the cheerleaders.

At that point one of three things would probably happen:

- Your life value of community would go out the door as your motivator of fame takes over and you would begin to compete with the person who is getting all the attention.

- Your motivating value of fame would be ignored and your life value of community would move you to focus on the performance of the entire team, not just on getting attention.

- You become caught in the dyadic energy of the conflicting values and lose your focus *and* your motivation to play your best.

Motivating values and life values that are in conflict may only create small annoyances, or they may result in huge, warring energies that are powerful enough to stop your forward progress dead in its tracks. Keep in mind that even a little bit of diffused energy and loss of focus caused by small conflicts between your motivating values and your life values will pile up when they're encountered on an ongoing basis, causing them to grow into a major blockage.

In this next exercise you'll be able to see if there are any conflicts between your life values and your motivating values.

Begin by listing your motivators in the space on the left side, using the motivators you identified previously. Then refer to your list of life values and, in the appropriate spaces, write those that are in alignment with each motivating value and those that are in conflict with them.

Motivating Value	Aligning Life Value	Conflicting Life Value
1.		
2.		
3.		
4.		
5.		

What new awareness have you gained about what motivates you and how it relates to your life values?

Words of Motivation

In addition to motivating values, there are also words that will attract or repel you. These words are all verbs — action words. The curious thing about these words is that, on the surface, all of them appear to be motivating action words. However, some of them will have the exact opposite affect on you. Instead of moving you into action, some of these words will stop you in your tracks, or worse, repel you backwards and away from what you desire.

Much like motivating values, everyone can be affected differently by the same motivating verb. You may feel very motivated by the word "dare," while that same word might scare the heebie jeebies out of someone else. "Have to" may motivate you, but may make your best friend absolutely comatose.

Whether you're stating a goal, an intent, or your next step, it's important to know which words are most effective for you. If you use the wrong words on yourself, you'll end up un-motivating yourself. Consciously choosing the words you use for motivation when talking and thinking about what you intend to do can make the difference between moving into action to achieve your intent or stopping you from moving at all.

Each of the motivating words listed in this exercise will have an emotional impact on you. Some words will have a stronger impact than others while some may even seem to be neutral. Use each one in a sentence that involves some task that you find despicable, such as "I must eat my brussels sprouts" or "I must clean the litter box." State it out loud use the same sentence throughout the exercise, changing *only* the motivational word or phrase. Use all the motivational words in the list and feel free to add any of your own that aren't listed.

As you read each one, wait for a moment afterward to get a sense of whether it attracts you and makes you want to move into action or whether it repels you and sets up resistance. Then, rate each of the following words on a scale from 1 to 10, with ten being a go-go-go motivational word and one making you want to dig your heels in or even to run in the opposite direction.

When you've chosen a number for a motivating word, insert that number right after the word and *before* the forward slash. Remember, you can add any motivational words of your own.

must ___/___	can ___/___	deserve ___/___
have to ___/___	may ___/___	should ___/___
intend ___/___	ought to ___/___	am able ___/___
supposed ___/___	do ___/___	dare ___/___

decide ___/___	need to ___/___	wish ___/___
let ___/___	allow ___/___	permit ___/___
want ___/___	could ___/___	will ___/___
choose ___/___	would ___/___	am ___/___
get to ___/___	might ___/___	better___/___

Now use each of the motivational words in a sentence with a task that's not only detestable, but is impossible to accomplish, such as "I have to paint the entire house today." Again, rate your response — this time inserting the number *after* the slash mark.

Review how you've rated these words. Circle the motivational words that rated the highest with you and list the top five below:

1.
2.
3.
4.
5.

Use these words when creating affirmations, intents, to-do lists, and any other tasks or goals.

Which did you rate the lowest? List them here.

1.
2.
3.
4.
5.

Vow *never ever* to use these words.

When stating your intent to move into action *always* choose words that work best for you as motivating words. Whether you state your intent out loud to someone else or just think it to yourself, always use words that support you in moving into action.

Miscellaneous Motivators

In the last chapter, we discussed lists and timeline charts. Here are some of the ways in which you can use these tools as wonderful motivators:

> **Lists:** Crossing a task off your to-do list is not only very satisfying, it motivates you to tackle another item on your list so that you can experience that wonderful sense of satisfaction again. Each time you accomplish something, you experience the pleasing sensation of success, and there's nothing like that feeling to create a desire for more of the same. It's like the snowball effect. As a snowball rolls downhill, it gathers snow and gets bigger and bigger. As you roll along, crossing off items on your list, you'll get more and more motivated to complete the remainder of the items.

> **The Timeline:** Keeping track of your progress is a wonderful motivator. As you chart your progress on a timeline, you'll gain a sense of accomplishment. Each day on your timeline will bring progress, and the visual image of your progress is not only rewarding, it will motivate you to continue forward.

Chart your path and keep track of your progress. Otherwise you may feel that you're on a continuum — which could be exactly what's happening. You may be creating movement, but it'll be like walking on a treadmill: a continuum of moving while staying in the same place and never making any forward progress.

The Greatest Motivator of All: Anger

When you become angry, you create one of the most powerful energies that exist on this planet that we humans have been given to work with.

Although powerful, the energy of anger isn't bad, negative, or harmful. Neither is it good, beneficial, or positive. It has no intent or purpose. Anger simply exists as energy.

All energy is neutral. What you choose to do with it determines if it's bad or good. As with any energy, you can choose to use it in harmful ways or in beneficial ways.

Fire, like anger, is an energy that you have the ability to create. Once created, some beneficial uses of fire may be to heat your home, cook meals, or toast marshmallows for S'mores. That same energy can be used in harmful ways, such as malicious arson in which the intent is to burn down a building. Fire is simply energy, and what determines whether it's good or bad, harmful or beneficial, is how you choose to work with it.

The same is true of the energy of anger. Once created, it can be used in ways harmful to others or yourself, or it can be used for the greatest benefit for all concerned.

An important fact to note about energy is that it's perpetual. Once created it cannot be destroyed. It can, however, be transformed. As energy is used, the chosen use determines whether it will be transformed into beneficial or harmful energy.

So, once you have created the energy of anger, you have choices about how to use this energy.

You can stifle your energy and stuff it inside yourself. But remember, the energy you've created is perpetual. It won't go away simply because you're keeping it inside you. What it *will* do is lodge itself somewhere in your body and create disease. The common question, "What's eating you?" is a question with an underlying truth in it. It refers to anger being stored in a person; anger that is, no doubt, eating away at their internal parts. High blood pressure, ulcers, colitis, stomach and intestinal cancers, and other digestive diseases are common in people who keep their anger stuffed inside themselves.

You can use your anger to create more anger. When you give voice to your anger, such as telling everyone you know the story of what that so-and-so did to you, you share not only your words. You share the energy of your anger as well.

This is not to say that talking about an incident that angered you is wrong. It's the *intent and purpose* of your discussion that determines whether it becomes beneficial or harmful. Talking with someone who can assist you in discovering a solution to the incident will help you transform the energy of your anger into the beneficial energy of positive action. When you handle your anger in this manner, you transform its energy into a beneficial energy through deeper understanding about the source that created it, thereby creating a solution to correct it.

However, when you use the energy of anger for simply complaining, you *grow* the potential harm of it by dispersing it to others in an untransformed state.

You can vent your anger with hard physical activity. Chopping wood, running, and working out are all activities that transform the energy of anger into physical energy, which is beneficial to you *and* your body. Toxins are produced in your body whenever you experience stress and some are released only through sweat. You can release these toxins by using the energy of anger to motivate you into working so hard you sweat. As you work out, you'll also be gaining the benefit of a stronger, healthier body. Transforming the energy of anger into physical energy not only is beneficial to your state of mind, it's also beneficial to your body.

You can choose to use the energy of anger to motivate you into creating a better situation. *This* is the highest purpose for anger. *This* is why we were given this emotion.

The energy of anger is the greatest motivator of all.

You have the opportunity to use this powerful energy to create something better out of the situation that created the anger in the first place. It's an opportunity for healing, which is the basis of your life purpose.

An example of using the energy of anger for healing might be a woman who is experiencing difficulties at work with one of her co-workers who undermines and belittles her. As she becomes angry, she can choose to use her anger for its highest and best purpose — as motivation to heal. She may choose to look more closely at exactly what she's getting angry about. As a result of this process, she may discover how she has chosen to be a victim and has been giving her power away to the co-worker. This may lead her to see that her victim behavior shows itself in other facets of her life, as she becomes aware of how she gives her power away to others as well. She might then choose to set personal boundaries that will garner for her the respect she desires.

As a result of transforming the energy of her anger into the highest possible use for which it was intended — *motivation to improve the situation that created it* — she'll enjoy a higher quality of life.

Groups such as MADD, NAACP, SPCA, Moveon.org, ERA, Greenpeace, and many others all began because someone got angry at a situation and chose to use the energy of their anger to transform the situation into something beneficial.

Transforming the Energy of Your Anger

Look deeply into a situation that you're currently experiencing or have experienced in the past that created anger within you.

Describe it briefly here:

What are some ways you might use this energy in order to change the situation into one in which everyone concerned would benefit? What do you think is the highest and best purpose of your anger in this situation?

1.

2.

3.

4.

5.

Select one action and do it within 24 hours. When you've completed it, note the transformative results here:

Manifesting

Manifesting is a word that's used more often and in many varied circumstances in recent years. In some instances, it may even seem to have taken on the attributes of some kind of magical practice. But what does it really mean?

Manifesting is simply using all your creative resources to bring forth a desired result.

In its most simple form, manifesting is nothing more than focusing your thoughts on what you want. The more you think about something, the more you train your brain to be on the lookout for anything resembling it. When it spots something similar to what you want, it alerts you. It's like the New Car Syndrome. If you buy a particular color and style of car, suddenly you see the same car everywhere — on the freeway, in parking lots, at the mall, in car lots.

Your brain will assist you in recognizing opportunities that could lead you to your desired goal. It may seem that whatever you focus on, you draw to you. Actually, what happens is that whatever you focus on activates the subconscious part of your brain to be on the lookout for anything resembling your desire. It sorts all incoming data, mostly visual and auditory, into either one of two categories: *like* what you're focusing on or *unlike* it. It then sends this information to the conscious mind, bringing to your awareness the things that are like your focused desire and directing your awareness away from anything dissimilar.

Everything that was ever created by a human was once a thought.

The good news about this is that you have the ability to create your future with the thoughts you're thinking now.

The bad news about this is that you have the ability to create your future with the thoughts you're thinking now.

You are the creator of your life. You create it with your thoughts, and the thought you're thinking right now is creating your future. That future may be the next moment or the rest of your life.

What are your thoughts focused on right now? Are you thinking about how many bills you have to pay? Well, guess what you're going to create? Right. More bills.

To fortify your creative manifesting powers, add emotion to your thoughts. So if you want to create even more bills, simply add worry, fear, or some other similar emotion, and you'll get *lots* of bills.

Want to create financial security in your life? Then think about how you've always managed to pay your bills, make the mortgage payment or rent, buy food (you haven't starved to death yet, have you?), and buy clothes to wear. Want to bring in even more financial security? Add the emotion of gratitude to your thoughts. Be grateful for your bills. After all, they represent the trust and faith that others have in your ability to create the money with which to pay them.

The condition of your life right now was not caused by your mother, father, boss, life mate, God, where you were born, or how you were raised. You have gotten to where you are now by the kajillions of thoughts that loop endlessly and continually in your brain every day.

The first step in consciously creating the future you want and manifesting it, is to become aware of the thoughts that are contained in that endless chatter flowing ceaselessly through your mind. With or without your awareness, these thoughts are designing your life.

What's on Your Mind?

What have you been thinking about some of the most important aspects of your life, such as your job, your friends, your happiness? If you have difficulty answering that question, find out what your thought-loops are by completing the following statements *with the first thoughts you have* as you read them. Do it as quickly as possible, not allowing your inner critic time to argue with you or correct what you first wanted to write down:

I think my job/work/career is:

I think my home is:

I think my money is:

I think the value of my work is:

What thoughts were surprises to you? Which seemed as familiar as an old t-shirt you've worn until it's all raggedy? Which of your thoughts are fear based and *not* what you want to use as you manifest your ideal future?

Now, circle all of the thoughts that represent what you *don't* want to create in your future. In the space below, turn their meaning around so they become thoughts that will manifest what you *do* want for your life.

1.

2.

3.

4.

5.

Celebrate!

After you've completed your list, celebrate the release of all these negative thoughts with a ceremony. You've just achieved a new level of awareness, which is a perfect reason to celebrate. Ceremonies are a fun way to mark your progress as you move toward your goal of living your life purpose.

Celebrate the release of the old, negative thoughts with a ceremony, such as:

- crossing out the fear-based thoughts in the exercise above with a brightly-colored crayon, red lipstick, or something else that's jazzy.
- writing the old, fearful thoughts on another piece of paper and burning it.
- noting the old thoughts on paper, and then gleefully ripping and tearing the paper into shreds.

Celebrate the creation and awareness of the *new* thoughts:

- use your computer to print them with an attractive font and hanging them on your wall as a mini-poster.
- frame the mini-poster in a beautiful frame, one that you'll love to look at.
- create a flag, pennant, or wall hanging with your new thoughts.

I AM

The I AM statement is enormously powerful language you can use in manifesting. When you use this statement, you're reinforcing to yourself who and what you believe you are. This statement also acts as a command to your higher self, your guides, and the Universe, who honor your I AM statement by assisting you to manifest it. If you're thinking, "I AM so depressed", your brain *and* your spirit guides will do everything in their power to manifest events and people to support you in that belief.

A very common, and almost unconscious, use of the I AM statement occurs when people meet. Almost automatically the question is asked, "How are you?" and just as automatically, the answer is given.

Your response to this query is a command to your conscious mind, subconscious mind, higher self, the Universe, and other spirit guides to create whatever you just stated. Your response creates this thought within the other person's mind too, enlisting the support not only of *their* conscious and subconscious minds, but also all of *their* spiritual forces in manifesting your I AM command. Now you have the power of two people *plus* all the spiritual forces helping to manifest your I AM statement.

For example, if you reply to the inquiry of "How are you?" with "I AM great," you not only reaffirm to yourself that you're great, but you engage the other person in thinking the same. You also call in all the forces to align you with who and what you just said you are — great.

Congratulations! You've just created your future and manifested greatness for yourself in a most powerful manner.

How do you typically respond to this question? Write your answer here:

What state of being would you like to manifest with the I AM statement?

Practice using the new and improved statement during the next few days each time you're greeted with "How are you?" Pay attention to how you feel after you've said it *and* to the reaction you receive from the other person.

I + A = M

This acronym may help you remember the power of the I Am statement each time you say or think "I am...":

Intention + Action = Manifestation

To see how you're now using this powerful statement, track your use of it during an entire day. You'll gain much clarity about how you're creating your life with your I AM statements.

Note each time you use it and what words follow I AM.
Statements such as "I AM going to do such and such" count, so
put them down, too.

I AM

I AM

I AM

I AM

I AM

I AM

I AM

I AM

I AM

I AM

What patterns, repetitions, or themes do you see in this
completed exercise?

What new awarenesses do you have about your thought habits?

Visioning

Have you ever thought about how you'd like to have something
and, within a short period of time, it seemed to appear as if by
magic?

It did appear by magic — the magic of visioning.

Actually, visioning isn't really magical, although it's rather fun to think so. There's a logical explanation behind the magic of using visuals for manifesting.

The part of your brain that's commonly called the conscious mind has an important function as a "sorter." Everything that comes into its awareness is judged and sorted into categories according to the criteria given it, such as whether something is safe for you or not. In order to do this, it must judge *everything*.

Coincidentally, this is also the part of your brain in charge of words and language.

The subconscious mind, on the other hand, is non-judgmental. It accepts as true all information that it becomes aware of. This is the part of your brain where images are stored.

Words are processed in your conscious mind where they're judged, while images are processed in your subconscious mind where they're not judged. Visualizing sends the message of whatever you want to create *directly* to your subconscious mind, bypassing your conscious mind. This eliminates any opportunity for critical judgment, which typically appears in the form of inner messages as to why you can't do something, like live your life purpose.

The judging process of your conscious mind has been variously named The Dreaded Inner Critic, The Gremlin, The Ego, Mr. Black Hat, the English Teacher, _____ (insert the name you use for this critical, judgmental voice). This negative character will tell you all kinds of reasons why you can't or shouldn't do something.

Try this experiment with your inner critic: using your inner voice, state your desire to do something, such as living an aspect of your life purpose. Then get ready for the barrage of reasons why you can't do it as your inner critic dumps on you. Now, visualize yourself actually doing some aspect of your life purpose. Listen… hear that? It's the silence of an absent inner critic.

A Recipe for Effective Visioning

Visioning is made even more powerful with the addition of a few ingredients. Here's a recipe for effective visioning:

> 1. With your inner vision, see the thing you want clearly. If it's an object, see every detail. If it's a value you want more in your life, see yourself experiencing this value. As an example, if it's a better relationship with your kids or mate, see yourself experiencing the fun, joy, and love that the better relationship will give you. You might envision playing with your kids at the beach and all of you laughing and having fun. You might envision you and your mate snuggling together and enjoying each other's company. Remember to make it as real and detailed as possible.

> 2. Now add sensory input. Smell, taste, feel, and hear all the associated aromas, flavors, textures, and sounds.
> 3. Feel the emotions that you'll be feeling when you have this thing you want. Is it joy? Excitement? Contentment? Whatever it is, add it into the mix.

> 4. Repeat often. Daily is recommended.

You might want to keep a journal of your visioning. Not only will it help you to remember all the details, it's also a great way to measure your progress and track the successes that you're manifesting.

Treasure Maps

Treasure maps, also known as goal setting posters and treasure collages, are powerful visualizing tools you can use to assist in manifesting your goal of living your life purpose. A treasure map is a collection of pictures — a collage — that represents your goals and has meaning for you.

The reason treasure maps work so well is because they use imagery, which bypasses the conscious mind where your inner critic, Gremlin, ego, or whatever-you-want-to-call-it lives. The symbolic imagery of a picture is sent directly to your subconscious mind, with no stops in the conscious mind. It's sort of like a direct flight with no layovers. When you're viewing a picture, there are no words for one of those nasties to argue with... just pictures.

Your subconscious mind directs your conscious mind to notice things that are related to the images you have on your treasure map. You'll see and recognize the things, events, and people that are opportunities to help you toward your goal. Without programming your subconscious to search for these things, you'd probably not even notice them and would likely pass them by. A familiar example of this is your awareness of how many cars there are yours You probably didn't notice them until after you made the decision to buy one, but now you see them everywhere.

Here are a few guidelines to creating an effective treasure map:

- In order to be of the utmost effectiveness, the images

on your treasure map should be meaningful to you.

• The images should impart to you a positive message and represent something that you want, not something you don't want. Remember, you create what you focus on. If you put pictures of credit cards on your treasure map because you want to pay off your credit card debt, what you'll end up with are *more* credit cards and *more* credit card debt.

• Words can be added for emphasis, but it's the pictures that have the power.

• The more often you view your treasure map, the more firmly embedded the images become in your subconscious mind. Post your treasure map where you will look at it often — optimally where it will be within your direct or peripheral vision most of the day. Putting it on the back of a closet door and peeking at it once a day will not be as effective as having it on a wall facing you as you work all day long. The more time that your subconscious has to assimilate the images on your treasure map, the quicker you'll see the items on it being manifested.

• The treasure map is to assist *you* in manifesting *your* goals and desires. It's not possible to do this work for others, no matter how much you love them. If you really want to help them, invite them to your treasure map party and give them the opportunity to create their own.

Treasure maps are one of my favorite manifestation tools, and I've witnessed many success stories through the years that I've been using them and teaching others how to use them. Here are a few examples:

During my annual New Year's Day Treasure Map Party, one of my friends created a treasure map with a picture of a wedding ring on it. A few weeks after the party, she called me excitedly to invite me to her wedding and to tell me about her wedding ring, which was *exactly* the same as the one in the picture she had cut out and put on her treasure map.

One year during my real estate career, I had pictures of some pretty big goals represented on my annual treasure map, such as a trip to Australia, windsurfing in Hawaii, a new computer, a horse with a long list of specifications (I had been looking for five years for this horse), and the man of my dreams. I put my treasure map on the wall in front of my desk where I would see it constantly. That year I got *everything* on my treasure map, including the man of my dreams, who is now my husband.

Another of my clients put a map of Italy on her treasure map, even though she had no particular desire to go there. She just wanted to travel. Six months later she called me to tell me she had been offered a trip to Italy with a friend of hers, *all expenses paid*.

And there are a lot more of these success stories. But instead of me telling you about all the success stories I know regarding treasure maps, how about you creating some successes of your own?

How to create a treasure map

What you'll need:

- **Poster paper.** Go to your local art supply store or stationers and buy some paper that is at least 18" x 24". You'll need something that big because you'll be filling it up with pictures faster than you think possible.

- **Magazines.** If you don't have old magazines lying around the house that have the types of images you want, ask friends for their old magazines, go to thrift stores and buy a bunch from them, go to the grocery store and buy the ones you want, and ask your doctor or dentist for some of their old magazines.
- **Glue.** Glue sticks work best. Less mess.
- **Scissors.** There are some that cut scalloped edges, zigzags, and all kinds of fun patterns.
- **Stickers, glitter, and other fun things.**
- **Colored pens or crayons,** just in case you want to emphasize something or write your own messages on your treasure map.

Once you have all your materials together, you're ready. You'll need lots of room to spread out, so the best place for creating a treasure map is on the floor. Don't worry about being tidy — creativity thrives in chaos. You can always clean up later. Have fun and free your creative spirit!

When you're done with your treasure map, give it more power by showing it to someone you know who supports you *one hundred percent* in your endeavor of living your life purpose. Share with them what each of the images represents to you in regard to your goal. As you do so, you'll be enlisting their support, both conscious and subconscious, *and* the support of all their spiritual forces.

Now, put your treasure map in a place where you'll see it often. Remember, the more often you see it, the more it will be embedded in your subconscious mind.

Don't be overly concerned with what other people, such as co-workers or family members, will say. Once you tell them what it is, they'll probably want one of their own!

Have a Treasure Map Party

It's great fun to do this with other people. You might want to do it with a friend or throw a party and invite lots of friends. If you're in business, consider inviting your employees, associates, and suppliers to a treasure map party.

One of the advantages, besides multiplying the fun, is that the power of each of treasure map is multiplied exponentially because everyone shares the meaning and symbolism of their treasure maps with each other. So, if you have a treasure map party with ten other people, the power of each treasure map will be multiplied by ten.

Every year I host a New Year's Day Potluck and Treasure Map Party. I supply big sheets of drawing paper, glue sticks, scissors, and a pile of magazines. Everyone brings more magazines and a dish or snack of some sort. We add their magazines to the pile I already have on the floor.

After everyone has had time to greet each other and get something to eat and drink, we begin creating our treasure maps with the goals and wishes of what we want to achieve in the upcoming year.

As each person completes their treasure map they stand up, hold their treasure map in front of them, and tell everyone what each of the images represents to them. They receive applause as well as words of support and encouragement from everyone.

If you've never done a treasure map, do it and get ready for fun *and* powerful manifesting!

You can have more than one treasure map too. They can be created for any specific goals or items you want:

- Goals for the upcoming year
- Specific things, such as a new house, car, or job
- Vacations
- Business
- Financial goals
- Relationships
- .

Affirmations

Another way to use your subconscious mind to help create what you want in life is to use affirmations. This is not magic; it's science. The fact that your brain can be reprogrammed has been proven by hypnotherapists all over the world. Behavioral psychologists have told us for years that it takes approximately 28 days to create a new habit. In other words, in less than a month you can reprogram your brain.

Affirmations are one method among many for reprogramming your brain to assist you in achieving your goals. Each time you repeat an affirmation, an order is sent to your brain, telling it to focus on looking for whatever you're affirming. For example, if you have affirmations that relate to increasing your good health, you'll find yourself almost automatically drawn to eating food that's better for your body. When you're in the grocery store your brain will bring your awareness to the fresh vegetables and how yummy they look. Before you know it, there you are, buying and eating healthful veggies!

Here's a bit of information about your brain that may help you to better understand how affirmations work: *your brain works only in the present and doesn't know the difference between now, yesterday, or tomorrow.*

If you were to think about what you did yesterday, your brain would bring the information about what you did yesterday *into the present time.* It doesn't go back in time to yesterday; it simply brings the archived information into the present. This works much like your computer does when it retrieves information that's stored in the memory on the hard drive and then displays it on the screen. All time is the present to a computer — and to your brain.

When you use affirmations to tell your brain that you've already achieved your goal, it accepts the information as true because it has no sense of time other than the present.

The power of affirmations is in wording them correctly to achieve the most effective reprogramming of the data in your brain. Here are four basic guidelines for creating affirmations:

> **1. Word them in present tense.** Creating an affirmation that begins with "I will have" or "I want to have" tells your brain that you want the object of the affirmation, not that you now have it. It places the achievement of what you want at some vague time in the future. Even though the affirmation may not be true at the present time, and it probably isn't or you wouldn't be creating an affirmation for it, *you must craft the wording of your affirmation as if it is true right now.* This is necessary for reprogramming your brain. As an example: "I now enjoy a healthy and loving relationship with my family."

2. Word them positively. Your subconscious mind doesn't recognize a negative, such as "no" or "not." To show you how this works, do not think of a purple elephant. You just envisioned a purple elephant, didn't you? The affirmation "I do not smoke cigarettes" will be recognized by your brain as "I smoke cigarettes." A better way to word this affirmation might be "I am free from smoking cigarettes."

3. Write them down. Although speaking them aloud adds power to affirmations, writing affirmations on paper and posting them someplace where you can read them often is much more effective. To make them still more effective, record your affirmations on tape and then listen to your own voice saying them as you read them.

4. Display them prominently so that you see them often during the day. The more often you see your affirmations, the more embedded they will become in your subconscious mind. They don't have to be in your direct line of vision — peripheral vision is just as effective as direct vision.

You can get as fancy or as basic as you want with style. In my office, I have some of my affirmations printed in beautiful fonts on colored paper, framed and hanging on the wall next to my computer. Other affirmations are scribbled on sticky notes and stuck on my filing cabinet and on my computer monitor. Neither style is more effective than the other, but one is most certainly more attractive!

In the space below, craft three affirmations that will assist you in obtaining your goal.

1.

2.

3.

Gratitude and Appreciation

Everything that you've manifested in your life has been created with the assistance of your spiritual guides, the Universe/Spirit/ God, your higher self, and other beings of Light. These beings are not so different from you in one respect — they all like to have their efforts appreciated.

Have you ever given a gift or a compliment to someone who never thanked you? No doubt you were much less willing to be so nice to them the next time. The same is true for your angels and other spirit guides who assist you in manifesting. If you want them to eagerly help you again, a little gratitude on your part will go a long way toward encouraging them to repeat their assistance.

Beyond encouraging your spirit guides to help you again, there's another very important reason to voice your thanks. Typically, when you tell someone "thank you," it's *after* you've received something from them — a gift, a kind word, a promise to do something for you. When you say "thank you" to your spirit guides before you receive what you're asking for, you're affirming that whatever you've asked for is already yours, is on its way to you, or it's already happened.

In the form of vibrational healing work that I do, part of the protocol is to give thanks for the healing *before my client and I witness that it's been done.* The reason for this is to show our gratitude and appreciation to the spiritual helpers as well as announcing to everyone involved that the healing is complete. When pre-thanks are given for the healing, the power of everyone involved, including the client's body, their conscious and subconscious minds, and their spirit guides, is focused on the belief that the healing is already complete. This adds immensely to the effectiveness of the healing.

Formulated in present tense and as if they are complete, affirmations are a form of acknowledging that the manifestation is already done, as in "I now have my red Jaguar convertible. Thank you." Voicing gratitude is one more way of accelerating your manifestation and bringing the future into the now.

Also, gratitude and appreciation are another way of focusing on that which you want in your life, and *not* what you don't want. As you know by now, what you focus on, you manifest. This is the prime reason that affirmations are formulated in a positive context of what you *do* want, not what you don't want.

Your Gratitude and Appreciation Journal

Keep a daily journal of everything that you're grateful for in a binder or spiral-bound notebook. List at least 15 things per day that you appreciate having in your life, whether you actually do have it in your life that day or not. Do it first thing in the morning so that it sets your energy for the day, much like aerobic exercise for 20 minutes will increase your metabolism all day. You'll find as you work through your list that your energy will rise as you identify all the things you're grateful for in your life.

Note the date at the top of each daily journal. Once a week look back through them and notice:

- how quickly you were able to manifest the things you were giving thanks for but didn't have yet.
- how the things you did have and were grateful for were amplified or multiplied.
- how much better you feel just reading about all the things you have in your life to be grateful for.

I'm grateful for you, and appreciate you as you travel forward on your journey of living your life purpose.

Notes:

Your Personal Support System

As you travel along the path toward living your life purpose, there will be many times when you'll want — and need — support. You might want comfort, encouragement, brainstorming, or someone to help with the paperwork. Whatever form of support you want or need, it's best to have a system in place *before* you need it.

The focus of this chapter is just that — setting up your personal support system so that whenever and wherever you would like support, you can instantly receive it.

A solid support system will keep you moving forward on your path, helping you around the detours, over the bumps, and through the chuckholes.

Even if you have a personal support system now, during this chapter you'll refine the quality and quantity of your system and the types of support that you get from it. When you're doing the work of your life purpose, not only do you deserve the best kind of support, you *need* it. There will be times when your work will be quite challenging, and without a strong support system in place the work will be unnecessarily more difficult. A proper support system can mean the difference between achieving your goal of living your life purpose or being overcome with difficulties and hardships — maybe even to the point of giving up. A strong personal support system guarantees that won't happen.

As you'll discover, not everyone you know qualifies for a place in your support system. Further, those who are already in your system may be designated for special types of support. Just as you have friends who seem to fall into certain categories — friends from work, family friends, friends who share a hobby or interest with you — effective support systems are categorized as well. Once you have clarity about what you want and who goes where, you'll know instantly which of the members of your support system will be the most appropriate choices for you to call on to receive exactly the support you want and need.

Asking for Support: The Fine Art of Delegation

There's no rule or law that says you have to do it all by yourself. You're not the only person on this planet, you know. There are others who are just waiting for you to ask them to assist you, to help you lighten your load as you travel along your path to living your life purpose.

Yes, I know, it's hard to ask for help. There's your pride to be considered, after all.

Here's something that may shift your beliefs about asking for help. Take a moment and think back to a time when you helped someone. How did you feel afterward? Your answer is probably something like, "I felt so happy to be able to help them and to do some good" or "It warmed my heart to be able to help them." Helping other people feels sooooo satisfying and fulfilling. *Would you deny your friends and loved ones an opportunity to feel that good about themselves by rejecting their offer of help?*

The next time you're reading a book, this one or another, remember that the book didn't become reality by one person doing all the work. Anyone who has written a book will tell you that they had *many* helping hands along the way to get it from being thoughts inside their head to becoming a real book. The author may write the book alone, but after that they have the help of many people such as book designers, publishers, editors, publicists, distributors, all the people who sell the book at the bookstores, plus all their friends and family who put up with them during the process. There isn't a book in existence that doesn't have at least one page of acknowledgments from the author, thanking all the people who helped to make the book possible.

So it is with you. Look around. There's an abundance of people who are willing to help you. *Now* is not the time to be shy or coy or to diminish yourself or your work. These people were put in your path at a specific time and a specific place so they can assist you. You contracted with most of them before you were birthed onto this planet just so they could help you. Some of them are simply gifts from the Universe. As you journey into living your life purpose you'll have ample opportunity to have others help you along your path.

Consider this: by allowing others to help you, you may just be helping *them* to live their life purpose. The graphic artist who designs beautiful book covers may be living his life purpose of creating beautiful, healing artwork. The publisher may be living

171

her life purpose by being a facilitator for others to share their inspirational and uplifting message.

The next time you're feeling overwhelmed or you simply don't want to do it all by yourself, remember what a gift you're giving others when you ask them to help you.

Deciding How and When to Delegate

The most opportune time to get some clarity about when and what you can release to others for their support is *before* you're lying flat out on the floor with a severe case of exhaustion or overwhelm from trying to do everything all by yourself. Here are some indications that it may be time to delegate:

> 1. When you feel resistance or reluctance when you think of performing a portion of the work.
> 2. When you're faced with something that you think you can do, but aren't proficient at doing.
> 3. When the work will go faster, easier, or be more fun with someone else to help.

If you experience difficulty in deciding whether you should delegate or do it yourself, use the following tests to aid you in making your choice.

The "Time to Hire a Professional" Test

This test is another tried-and-true method to determine if it's appropriate for you to activate your option of delegating. It works like this: estimate how long it will take you to do something, *including the time you'll need to spend learning how to do it if you don't already know how.* Multiply that by what you earn per hour at your livelihood now. Then get an estimate from a professional. Compare the two bottom line numbers.

Here's an example. My neighbor can change the oil in his truck. It takes him 2 hours @ $25 per hour (his current wage) plus the cost of the oil and filter (about $30). Two hours of his time equals $50 plus $30 for materials makes a grand total of $80. *Or* he can take it to one of those quick lube places and have it done in 15 minutes for $35.

He does it: 2 hours/$80.
Quick lube does it: 15 minutes/$35.

Being an intelligent person, he delegates the job to the quick lube place.

The "Can and Want" Test

Delegation is another method of prioritizing. Previously you learned about prioritizing *things* such as chores, tasks, appointments, etc. Delegation is about prioritizing *who* the most appropriate person is to do a particular piece of work — you or someone else.

In addition to The Time to Hire a Professional Test, another method for deciding who would be the best person to do the job is the "Can and Want" Test. While you're doing this exercise, don't be concerned about to whom you're actually going to delegate. You'll do that later. For now focus on *what* you want to delegate.

List up to 10 things that need to be done according to one of your charts — the flow chart, the timeline, or your mind map. If you choose your mind map, you may want to use just one branch instead of the entire map.

1.
2.
3.
4.
5.
6.
7.
8.
9.
10.

Item by item, decide if it is something you *can* do or not. "Can" means you have the physical ability *and* the knowledge to actually do it. When you've decided if you can do the item or not, write it under the appropriate heading below:

	I can do this:	I'll delegate this:
1.		
2.		
3.		
4.		
5.		
6.		
7.		
8.		
9.		
10.		

From the "I can do this" category, choose what you *want* to do, or are at least *willing* to do. Be particularly sensitive to any feelings of resistance as you review each item. If the word "should" appears in any of your thoughts as you read an item, move it to the "I'll delegate this" column.

	I want to do this:	I'll delegate this:
1.		
2.		
3.		
4.		
5.		
6.		
7.		
8.		
9.		
10.		

That whittled the to-do list of yours down some, didn't it? Often when a plan as grand as your life purpose is created, it can be overwhelming in its magnitude. Selecting what you can and will delegate lessens the burden of the total workload and is a wonderful way to enlist the aid of your support system members. Understanding and using the art of delegation is a very effective way to enable you to travel lightly on your path as you live your life purpose.

The Support You Want

Remember a time when you were having trouble of some sort and your friends stood by you and supported you? Maybe you needed comfort and they gave you a hug or a shoulder to cry on. Maybe you needed help with a project and they rolled up their sleeves and jumped right in to help you with your work. Maybe you needed encouragement when you thought you couldn't go one more step and they became your personal cheerleader. Or maybe your experiences with asking and getting support were less than what you wanted. Maybe you needed comfort and they rolled up their sleeves to help you with the physical labor, or you wanted to celebrate a win and they gave you a critique of your performance.

When you ask for support, it's important to do two things:
1. Know first of all what type of support you want before you ask.
2. Ask specifically for the type of support you want.

None of the people in your support system are capable of giving you *all* of the multitudinous types of support you may want. They're only human after all. It's only fair to fit the right support person to the right job... and to let them know what that job is. If you don't, you may get cheerleading when you want muscle.

This story about a coaching client serves as a graphic example of why your results will be better when you're clear about what you want and ask specifically for it.

My client was upset because she was going through a very stressful time and wasn't getting the support she desired from her two sisters. According to her, she was always the one who offered support to her sisters, but she was never on the receiving end of support. When I asked if she had *ever* gotten support from them in any form, she recalled a time when she was moving and one of them, Sister #1, came to help. When I asked if Sister #2 had helped during this move, she replied that she hadn't. After some thought, however, she did remember a time when she was going through a stressful situation at work, and Sister #2 was right there with emotional support.

After some reflection of a few more instances, she came to the awareness that Sister #1 was great at helping her physically, but had little or no capability for emotional support, while Sister #2 was just the opposite and was always available for emotional support. She was delighted that she now knew which sister to turn to for the type of support they were best capable of giving her. No longer would she go to Sister #2 to ask for help painting her house, nor would she ask Sister #1 to comfort her when she was going through emotional situations.

The right support person for the right job! Works every time!

What kinds of support do you want from the people on your personal support system? Advice? Non-judgment? Encouragement? Belief in you? Muscle? Whatever forms of support you would like, list them here. Use additional paper if you run out of space.

1.
2.
3.
4.
5.
6.
7.
8.
9.
10.
11.
12.
13.
14.
15.

Which of your life values showed up on this list?

The People in Your Personal Support Team

Now that you know *what* you want from your Personal Support Team, you're ready to create a list of *who* you want in it. In the space below, list at least ten people whom you want in your team. If you have more than ten people, use another sheet of paper.

1.
2.
3.
4.
5.
6.
7.
8.
9.
10.

Now, refer to the types of support you listed in the previous exercise. After each name note which type of support each person is willing *and* able to give you. Some may only be available for one form of support, while others may be able to give you multiple forms of the support you want.

Three Levels of Support

Not only are there different types of support, there are also levels of support. It's important to know the type of support the people in your system are willing and able to give you, *and* it's important to know at what level they give their support. There are three basic levels of support:

> **Those who always support you unconditionally.** This means that no matter what you choose to do, they're behind you 100%.
>
> **Those who sometimes or conditionally support you.** Conditional support is just that — support with a condition attached. Example: a friend may support you in traveling to foreign countries, but only if you go with group tours and not by yourself.
>
> **Those who won't usually or never support you.** This level of support, or lack thereof, isn't always blatantly obvious. The people you place in this level are very valuable, but for another purpose, which you'll discover soon..

Unconditional Support

The first level of support is very rare. Few, if any, of the people you have on your list will always be able to give you this lofty level of support. Most people are not capable of *always* unconditionally supporting you no matter how much they love and respect you. There may be some on your list who are capable of giving you unconditional support sometimes or most of the time. But, remember that they have lives, too. Whatever is going on in their life may, at times, make them unavailable to you for this kind of support. This is a very good reason why you have more than one member in your support system, and more than one member in each level and type.

Conditional Support

Most of the people in your support system will fall in this second level of support. There are many reasons for support being conditional. Most have to do with the fact that the people in this level *do* love you and are, to varying degrees, fearful for your safety. What they perceive to be unsafe for you and what actually *is* unsafe for you may be two entirely different things, however. Remember that the support they give you is filtered through their own experiences and fears. If someone in your support system had a bad experience doing something similar to what you're proposing to do, you can expect to receive conditional support at best.

The condition attached to support may be valuable information that you haven't considered. Their caveats for support may be disguised forms of troubleshooting future potential problems. Before pooh-poohing their fearful conditions and dismissing them as silly, it might behoove you to examine them.

Non-Support
There are as many reasons as there are grains of sand on the beach why some people won't give you the support you want or need.

- The reason may be that at the present time they have something going on in their own life that renders them temporarily incapable of any type of support.
- It's possible that they may be unable to find it within themselves to support you in just this one particular instance.
- It may be that they won't support you — no matter what.
- These people may love you but have their own personal issues with what you're doing.
- They may be envious or jealous because, unlike you, they don't allow themselves to follow their passion.

- They may be doing something similar and see you as competition.
- They may have suffered a great disappointment in life and don't want to see you have the same miserable experience they had.

Whatever the reason and whatever the issues, the people at this level are incapable of supporting you.

How to Recognize Non-supporters

I can't emphasize enough how important it is to identify these people and to be careful around them when you're in the beginning stages of living your life purpose. During this time you'll be vulnerable and will need to protect yourself. You'll be making some big changes in your life and not everyone is going to be tickled with the way you're changing or what you're doing.

Often non-supporters are those who love you very much. It may seem like a contradiction that they would not lend you their whole-hearted support if they love you so much, but as you'll soon recognize, love and support don't necessarily follow one another.

Non-support typically comes in the following forms:

Criticism — usually unasked for and often couched with a softener, such as, "I'm only telling you for your own good." It's not. It's for *their* own good.

Put-downs and snide remarks — this is a favorite of passive-aggressive people. Usually it's followed by a statement like, "I was only kidding. Can't you take a joke?" The damage that can be done by this form of non-support is anything but funny.

Sabotage — sometimes physical, but most often verbal and emotional, this can take many forms. Examples of this type of non-support are someone making plans that conflict with your plans, and which seem more important, such as a family outing during the time you had set aside for your sacred creative time, or scheduling a meeting with clients during the same time slot you scheduled for working on your new project.

Guilt — this commonly comes from those closest to you and can be the most devastating form of non-support. One antidote for guilt is to divert it. Create a vision of how much more wonderful the non-supporter's life will be as you're living your life purpose and then share the vision with them — continually.

"Yes Buts" and "Except Fors" — these can be very subtle and often appear to be a form of support. Know this: *everything* that goes after the "Yes but" and the "Except for" negates whatever went before it, creating non-support. Make the "Yes buts," the "Except fors," and all their relatives your red alerts, warning you that non-support is coming your way.

Until you're strong enough, it's best if you don't talk to non-supportive people about what you're doing to move forward with your life. Let them talk about themselves, keeping the attention off you and your work until you have a foundation in place that's strong enough to withstand their non-support.

What to Do With Non-support

First, and most important, know that it's not about you. It's about them. Whoever is giving you their particular form of non-support is doing so because of their own fears, not because what you're doing is wrong, stupid, or dangerous. It only appears to be so to them as they view your actions through the filters of their own life experiences.

Understanding the reason for the non-supportive action can give you a new perspective and help to diffuse the pain of it. Often the cause of non-support is because the other person had a similar experience, which turned out to be unsuccessful for them and caused them much pain. Because they care about you very much they want to protect you from experiencing such pain. This is misguided support, since they have no way of knowing if you'll have the same experience they did.

Another common cause of people being non-supportive to you in your endeavor is having a low value of themselves, and therefore seeing you as competition. One of the basic truths of the Universe is that there's always enough for everybody. A friend of mine tells me that if the wealth of the world were shared equally with every man, woman, and child on the planet today, each would have $10,000,000. Yes, that's ten million dollars! Unfortunately, the people who refuse to support you because of their low self-esteem don't believe that there truly is enough. They believe that if you receive something, it was taken from someone else. You gain, they lose. And vice versa.

Personal Boundaries and Non-Support

Being in the presence of non-supportive people is an excellent opportunity for you to use your personal boundaries and create protection for yourself. Create your boundaries now, being absolutely clear about what you will and will not accept in regard to other people's behavior toward you during this vulnerable time, and you'll be well prepared when you're subjected to the venom of non-supportive people.

Whatever the reason for its occurrence, when you experience non-support, remember that it's not directed at you. It's actually directed right back at the source; you just happen to be mirroring to them the fear they're emitting. State your personal boundary calmly and ask for their compliance. Whether you receive it or not, know as you walk confidently away that their fear is *theirs*, not yours.

A Story of Non-Support

A very sad example of non-support occurred years ago during a meeting of a group I had organized called "Women in Transition." All the members were "of that certain age" and were shifting priorities from doing what was expected of us to what we loved to do.

One of the women had been in banking all her adult life and, because her husband had a physical handicap, was the sole support of their family. It was easy to see that she barely tolerated her work and felt no passion for it. During one of the first meetings, she shared with us that what she really wanted to be was a seminar leader. We encouraged her with unconditional support and she began to create her seminar. Her demeanor changed from being withdrawn and shrinking into herself to being excited, speaking with energy and enthusiasm, and seeming to be lit up from within. She was blossoming right before our eyes! A few weeks later she committed to giving a small presentation at the next meeting and everyone was looking forward to it.

When the next meeting rolled around, she had reverted to her old downcast self. We quizzed her as to what had happened that created this dramatic change. She finally confessed that she had told her sister, who professed to love her very much, about her plan. Her sister, as it turned out, was leading a life of frustration and was grudgingly resigned to her plight. She had lambasted our future seminar leader for being irresponsible and uncaring in her dream of living her passion. There was nothing we could say to bring back the life we had seen in our friend when she was planning on moving ahead with her life purpose. The damage had been done… and by one who apparently loved her dearly.

The moral to the story is this: know who will give you support and who won't, and know the type and level of support they are willing and able to give you. Julia Cameron puts it into words that are a bit stronger in her book, *The Artist's Way*. She says, "*Do not indulge or tolerate ANYONE who throws cold water in your direction. Forget good intentions. Forget they didn't mean it.*" Their good intentions may be covering up a fear that stopped them from living their life purpose and, if you allow it, will stop you from living yours as well.

The value of non-supporters

This level of support may not seem like it's worth anything, but after you've gotten far enough along on your journey of living your life purpose to have gained sufficient confidence, you'll discover it has great value. The folks at this level are very valuable to you as troubleshooters.

When you're far enough along with your plans that you want to find out what could possibly go wrong before it actually *does* go wrong, just ask one of them what they think of it. They'll be delighted to tell you in great detail everything about your plans that has even a remote chance of not working.

Some of these people are professionals, such as lawyers and accountants. They're experts at finding all the things within their realm of knowledge that could possibly go wrong. When you're at the stage of implementing your life purpose, or even before, you may want to ask these experts for their particular form of support so that you're prepared for possible problems that you couldn't possibly foresee.

Sorting Your Personal Support System

Review your list of people in your PST. Note in front of each name the level of support you can expect: unconditional, conditional, or non-support. For easy reference, you may want to use a different color of highlighter for each level — green for unconditional, yellow for conditional and red for the non-supporters.

You now have a Personal Support Team that's organized. Now you can instantly spot whom to ask for specific types and levels of support.

The One Scary Thing

The people that you've just identified as your Personal Support Team would serve no purpose if you never put them to work. When you find yourself faltering or beginning to slow down on your path to living your life purpose, remember that you have a

PST from which to draw strength, encouragement, and whatever else you want. All you have to do is ask. You'll be more apt to receive support if you ask for it rather than wait around for someone to intuitively guess that you need it.

The One Scary Thing exercise will give you experience in asking for and getting the support you want and deserve. Think of something that you want to do but that you're resisting because it's scary. Then complete this sentence:

The one thing I'm afraid to do is:

Now refer to your list of support people. Who might give you support to do this scary thing and help you over or around this obstacle?

Three people who will support me **unconditionally** in this are:

1.
2.
3.

Ask one or more of the people you just listed for their support in helping you to do the one scary thing. Help them help you by being as specific as you can about what you would like from them. Examples might be help with the wording on a proposal or their presence and handholding during a difficult phone call.

Three people who will support me **conditionally** in this are:

1.
2.
3.

Write next to their names any conditions they voice to you. They may be candidates who will support you in doing this one scary thing, as long as you understand and can accept their conditions.

Three people who **won't support** me in this are:

1.
2.
3.

DO NOT breathe a word of your plan to do this one scary thing to *anyone* you just placed on this last list. At a later time, you may want to use them to troubleshoot your plans, but for now you don't need their negativity. You need courage and support.

The Walt Disney Support System

Ol' Walt was not only a great cartoonist, he was one of the most amazingly creative people who ever walked on our planet. His creativity touched everything he did, including running his business.

He created an organization in which people were divided into three basic categories:

- **The Creatives:** artists, musicians, and writers.
- **The Realists:** people who implemented the ideas and creations of the Creatives. They figured out how to make the things that the Creatives envisioned.
- **The Troubleshooters:** people who found all the ways that the ideas of the Creatives wouldn't work. Now, you might think that these are the people you'd probably get rid of in your organization. But Walt knew their value.

The building which housed his company was on three floors: the highest one was where the Creatives worked, the second floor was where the Realists worked, and the bottom floor was where he kept the grounded Troubleshooters.

The Creatives were free to "keep their heads in the clouds" and be completely creative without having to concern themselves with how their creations might actually work. Walt didn't want to bog them down and stifle their creativity with anything so mundane as practicality.

Their creastions were then given to the Realists who would turn them into physical reality. These people might even be called upon to make a new piece of equipment to create a special effect that the Creatives had dreamed up.

Then the Troubleshooters (accountants and lawyers and such) were given the project to gnaw on and find all the weak spots. After they were satisfied that they had found all the things wrong with the project, it was given back to the Realists so that they could fix the weaknesses that had the potential to become large problems at a later date.

The Troubleshooters never had direct contact with the Creatives on a project. Walt knew that contact between those two groups would be fatal to the Creatives' spirit. Troubleshooters, being in the level of Non-supporters, can do irreversible damage to an infant idea or dream. Once the idea was formed, the Creatives were done with their work.

Remember, it was up to the Realists to make the vision into reality. After they were complete with their portion of the project, it was sent to the Troubleshooters for fine-tuning. If they found anything wrong, and of course they did because that's their life purpose, the details were sent back to the Realists for fixing. Never was anything returned to the Creatives, since that would have quelled their creative spirit and stifled their productivity.

Your Personal Support Team can be divided into these three types of people. As you move along your life purpose path, there will be times when you'll want help being creative, times when you'll want support in figuring out how to make your ideas work, and times when you'll want to know what problems might arise now and in the future so that you can be prepared for them or make plans to avoid them entirely.

Your Creative Stage

As you begin to live your life purpose, the first stage you'll be in is the creative stage — visioning, intuitively following your passions, being hit with inspirations. This is the time to surround yourself with people who are also creative. At this point, practical support people such as Realists will halt your creative flow. They have a tendency to focus their thinking on how a thing is going to work. They want to start planning, diagramming, and using timelines and flowcharts, rather than being open to letting the ideas and creativity flow. Realists are not ideal participants for a brainstorming session since brainstorming requires flowing with the creative process and allowing new ideas to emerge. It doesn't allow for stopping to figure out how ideas will actually work.

The *last* person you'd want to ask for creative support would be a Troubleshooter. The first idea you have would be shot down, its dead carcass full of holes from the smoking gun of the critical Troubleshooter. Do as Walt did and never let your Troubleshooters talk directly to your Creatives. Buffer both of them from contact with each other by the Realists.

Your Realist Stage

When you're complete with your visioning (at least for a while) then it's time to move into the stage of planning and implementing your ideas. The Realists will be of immense support during this stage because they simply *live* for this type of action. Tell them your dream and watch how quickly they whip out their spreadsheets and to-do lists. They'll also have an incredible list of resources for those things they're unable to do or to figure out.

Your Troubleshooter Stage

After your Realists have helped you figure out how you're actually going to make your plan work, the Troubleshooters are the next members of your Disney Support System that you'll want to consult. When you show them your plans, they're the ones who will say something like, "This will never work." When you ask why, you'll get a full explanation, such as, "Look here. You've got the doomaflingy connected to the whichamajingo and it'll short out the flootsit." They'll save you time, money, and energy by seeing faults that are, to them, obvious.

Creating Your Very Own Disney Support System

Just like Walt Disney, you can create your own three-tier support system using the people on your list of unconditional and conditional support people. Add the name of each person to the appropriate category below — Creative or Realist. While you're at it, make a check mark to note whether they will support you unconditionally or conditionally. As you're going through your list, you may discover that there are others who would make a great addition to your Disney support system. Feel free to add their names, too. (The non-supportive people aren't listed here because they automatically go into the category of Troubleshooters.)

Creatives   Unconditional/Conditional
1.
2.
3.
4.
5.

Realists   Unconditional/Conditional
1.
2.
3.
4.
5.

Your Personal Support Team

You now have a comprehensive Personal Support Team, filled with select friends and family whom you can call on for all the different types of support you might want as you travel along the path of your life purpose. You've prioritized and categorized the members so that you know whom you can safely contact to receive the type of support you want at the appropriate level.

Keep these lists handy for when you'd like some support as you journey toward living your life purpose. If you find that you're hesitant to call on one of the people in your support system, remember… you may be assisting them to live *their* life purpose.

Your Spiritual Support System

Beyond all the people in your life who are available for your personal support system, you have another multitude of support personnel who are ready, willing, and able to help you at a moment's notice. You have spirit guides, angels, devas, lightbeings, the Universe, your higher self, and millions more just waiting for you to ask them for help.

You may think that you haven't received any answers to your soul-driven questions about your life purpose, but indeed you have. One piece of evidence proving this is the fact that you are now reading these words. You were gently nudged by your spirit guides to pick up this book, open it, and begin reading. In their infinite wisdom, your guides knew that this book could be a valuable tool to assist you in your journey on the path of your life purpose.

Whether you decide that the information in this book is or isn't what you're looking for is not as important as the fact that you heeded your spiritual guidance by following your impulse. Paying attention to this kind of impulse is one of the many ways in which you honor the guidance you're given from your sources of higher wisdom.

You have many sources you can access to receive guidance and many ways to connect with these sources. You'll find some easier and more effective for you to use than others. This book is chock full of information and exercises to help you tune in to the higher wisdom that's available to you at all times.

There are many ways to recognize the guidance that you're constantly being given in order to nudge you toward your life purpose. You, like everyone else, have your own sources of higher wisdom and most effective methods of receiving guidance – even if you aren't aware of it. You don't need psychic powers in order to receive this information. *All you have to do is pay attention.*

It's rather like you're a radio, and the guidance is being transmitted on many different frequencies. When you learn what the many frequencies are, you can easily tune in to them, receive their broadcast, and clearly hear the messages that are being sent to you. You can even turn the volume up or down — *you're* in control.

There are many forms that spiritual support and guidance take as they appear in your life. Synchronistic events and serendipitous happenings are a couple of the most common — and the most fun. Don't you just love it when you ask for something, perhaps almost as a second thought, and before you know it you've gotten what you want?

One of my clients told me a story of how he had seen a most beautiful and rare edition of a book. He wanted it, but the book wasn't for sale. Weeks later he was wandering around a part of town in which his travels usually didn't take him, when he spotted a bookstore. On impulse, he went inside and was immediately stopped dead in his tracks by a vision of the book he wanted so dearly. It was in a special glass case, seemingly just waiting for him to come in and claim it. Yes, it was for sale and yes, he bought it.

Besides impulses, serendipity, and synchronicity, other forms of guidance you might receive can be:

- "gut feelings," goose bumps, tingling, or other bodily sensations
- emotions that shift instantly when you think of something or someone
- your inner voice speaking to you — not ordinary mind chatter
- animal messengers, which are different from everyday animals
- dreams, especially the kind that give you a "dream hangover"
- inner vision

If you only knew how much support you have from the unseen realms you would never doubt yourself and the path you're on. Your steps would be confident and sure always. But, you don't know, and that's what this chapter is all about.

Your Other Contracts

In addition to the Soul Contract you created before you were birthed onto this planet, you also created many contracts with others. Knowing that you would not remember who you truly

195

are and the work that you chose to do this lifetime, you set up the agreements with others who would help guide you to remembering your life purpose.

People who seem to walk into your life just when you need them are not there by accident. You requested assistance of them and they agreed to do help you. You and they formed a contract spelling out what you wished to experience and how they would assist you.

The experiences you requested may not always be pleasant or fun — for you *or* for those assisting you. Bless all those as they help you, in whatever form their help appears, for that is how you wished it. Their help and guidance may not always appear to you as kindness, generosity, and loving support. There may be people in your life you dislike for how they treat you. Bless them the most, for they give you the greatest gift of all. Those who are not pleasant to you are giving you gifts of immeasurable value, such as inner strength, integrity, or courage. You could not possibly gain these incredible gifts in any other way.

It takes a greater amount of love to be strict with children than it does to give them everything they want. If your parents made you get a job babysitting or delivering newspapers so that you could buy the bicycle or doll you wanted, they were fulfilling their contract with you. In your contract with them, you may have asked them to be strict with you so that you could gain knowledge of money flow. The knowledge you gained by being in business for yourself at such a young age might serve you well at a later time in life. You may also have wanted to learn something even more valuable, such as responsibility, achievement, pride of accomplishment, or honor.

Each person you connect with in your life is fulfilling their contract with you. You may have only a brief encounter with them, but during that connection you'll take away something that will be of value to you in your path to living your life purpose. What they give you may be something as seemingly unimportant as a single word. However, this word might be a trigger to open new pathways of thought for you, moving you along your path even faster, or maybe even redirecting you to another route that allows you to live your life purpose.

Remember a time when you were looking for a resource or an answer, and from the most unlikely encounter with someone, you received exactly the information you needed? The person could have been a complete stranger, someone you'll never meet again this lifetime, or maybe it was someone very close to you who said or did something so out of context for them it set you to wondering if aliens had taken over their body. That connection was a contract that both of you set up before your birth and which is now fulfilled.

As you travel along your path to living your life purpose, know that there are no unplanned incidents. All is in Divine order, just as you wished it.

Serendipitous Awareness

Serendipitous happenings are some of the most fun ways to receive guidance. As you begin to recognize them, you'll find they happen more often. So, let's get started with your serendipitous awareness.

For one entire day, pay attention to the people with whom you have an encounter. It may be in person, over the phone, or via email. List at least 15 of these people below. After each name, note briefly what happened in each encounter.

1.

2.

3.

4.

5.

6.

7.

8.

9.

10.

11.

12.

13.

14.

15.

Spend a few moments reviewing each of these encounters. What part of the conversation you shared with them might hold a message or guidance for you? Circle or highlight any key words or phrases.

How might that person be a response to a plea for help that you asked for, no matter how casually? What else do you see in any or all of these encounters?

Repeat this exercise again tomorrow, and the next day, and the next. Soon you won't need to make notes to recognize these messengers. You'll be spotting them as they happen.

Your Major Soul Contracts

Beyond the seemingly chance encounters you have every day with people — which you now know aren't by chance — there are the major Soul Contracts that have a great influence on you during this lifetime. These are long-term, highly involved relationships, such as your nearest relatives, friends, mates, and others with whom you are close.

Your request of these people was for them to interact with you during this lifetime at a deep level so that you would best be able to experience certain lessons. Both of you agreed what roles you would play, how you would act them out, and under what circumstances.

These people may not always appear to be acting out of love for you, but know this: *no one wants to be the villain.* Only someone who loves you very, very much would agree to be abusive to you simply because you asked them. Only someone who loves you in boundless amounts would agree to treat you badly so that you could learn what a particular experience is like and, thus, gain valuable qualities from it that will assist you in living your life purpose. Remember, it's at *your* request that they play their part.

A father who is physically abusive to his son may be fulfilling his part of their Soul Contract so that the son can gain compassion, inner strength, and unconditional love. The father might be learning from the son forgiveness, compassion, and humility. The mother who is overly strict with her daughter may be fulfilling her part of their Soul Contract so that the daughter might learn about structure, allowing, and responsibility. The mother may be learning about control and flexibility.

Although it may seem to you that some of these experiences are horrible, remember that it's only possible to learn about a thing by experiencing all facets of it. In order to learn completely about love, you must know all facets of it, including its opposite — fear. It's only possible to know safety by experiencing risk. It's only possible to learn completely about empowerment by being a victim.

The qualities you're learning through your relationships with other people are necessary for you as you live your life purpose. A doctor who hasn't learned compassion as well as the scientific aspects of medicine will not be capable of completely fulfilling his life purpose of healing people. He may cure their symptoms, but without compassion he'll never be able to heal the whole person. An artist who has not learned about structure will never be able to completely experience chaos, which is a necessary part of creating. Each relationship you have with another person offers you the gift of experiencing a quality you need in order to fully live your life purpose.

Your Soul Contracts

List five people who have been major influences in your life — good or bad. After each name describe briefly what your relationship was like and the gift that you gained from it.

1.

2.

3.

4.

5.

How do you imagine each of these qualities might assist you as you're living your life purpose? List each of the qualities and note how you see them being of value as you do your life purpose work.

1.

2.

3.

4.

5

Your Spiritual Support Team

What if you were told you have access to all the knowledge and wisdom that exists now and forever, and that you could access it instantly? Would you believe this to be true? Consider these items:

All thought exists as a form of energy. Each thought that you have creates energy. This is measurable and provable with the scientific and engineering miracle of an EEG.

Energy is perpetual. Once created, energy cannot be un-created, although it can be transformed into another form of energy. The written word, such as this book, was once the energy of thought, which was then transformed into the printed word, and is now being transformed once more into the energy of thought as you read it.

Energy is intelligent. Energy that once existed as thoughts of people such as Albert Einstein, Thomas Edison, Plato, and other geniuses, still exists in some form. You have the ability to tap into this energy and receive the knowledge and wisdom from it. If you think that's a far-fetched idea, consider this: do you pray for guidance from Jesus, Buddha, Allah, or the angels? If your answer is yes, then you're not only tapping into this same flow of energy, you're also communicating with it.

Your SST (Spiritual Support Team)

You have the ability to connect with the thoughtform energy of anyone who has ever lived on this planet. This means you have a

Spiritual Support Team that includes the likes of Thomas Jefferson, Deepak Chopra, Paramahansa Yogananda, Joan of Arc, and all the other great people who have ever lived on our planet.

If you could have anyone you wished on your Spiritual Support Team, who would it be? Create your team by choosing five people who may or may not be alive today. Remember, once the energy of their thoughtforms is created, it's available perpetually. In the space below, list five people you'll honor with a place on your SST.

1.

2.

3.

4.

5.

Why did you choose these particular folks? What are the qualities they have that you want in the people on your team? After each name, note the qualities that you admire in them.

Review what you've just written. Which of your life values are reflected in the qualities of these people?

The One Scary Thing... Again

Your Spiritual Support Team is a powerful resource that you can use any time you want to gain support as well as to access higher wisdom. You can tap into the wisdom of each of the people in your team to access their knowledge about any issue that you're currently facing.

In the previous chapter, you enlisted the aid of your Personal Support Team to help you through the One Scary Thing. Now you have the opportunity to get support and guidance from your Spiritual Support Team.

The following exercise will give you experience in using your imagination and intuition to ask for and receive the support and wisdom of your team. You may want to ask a friend or your life coach to assist you by taking notes of the conversations you'll be having with these wise people.

Complete this sentence: One thing I'm afraid to do is

Before you begin the exercise, get comfortable, take three nice, deep, relaxing breaths, breathing through the nose. When you feel clear and centered, begin.

Imagine that you're with your SST. Perhaps you're sitting on comfortable chairs in a circle or seated at a round table. Select one of the members and ask for any guidance that they'd like to share with you regarding your one scary thing. Perhaps you might ask how you can face this challenge with courage, how you can most easily accomplish it, or simply what advice they have for you. Talk to them freely and ask as many questions as you like, just as if they were truly sitting in front of you.

When you've received information from one of the members, write it down here, or have your assistant write it down, and then move on to the next one. Continue this process until you're complete with your conversations.

1.

2.

3.

4.

5.

What is the theme of everyone's information and advice to you on this issue?

You can change the members of your SST or add to them at any time. On occasion, you may want the expertise of only one person about a facet of your life purpose. At other times you may want a group of experts who specialize in one particular subject. It's your team to do with as you wish, and they exist solely to assist you along your path toward living your life purpose.

Remember, the wisdom of your Spiritual Support Team is available to you at any time. All you have to do is ask.

Your Fantasy Support Team

In addition to all the other support you have, there's also the Fantasy Support Team. These are people who have never lived — at least not physically. They've lived in our minds as the fantastic creatures they truly are. Characters such as Superman, Xena, Captain Kirk, and Bugs Bunny were all created using the energy of someone's thoughts and exist perpetually. You can access the wisdom they embody in the same way you access the wisdom of your Spiritual Support Team.

Who are some of your favorite fantasy heroes? List five of them here:

1.

2.

3.

4.

5.

What are the qualities that you admire most about them? Write these qualities after each name.

Which of your life values are reflected in the qualities that you admire in these heroes?

The One Scary Thing and Your Fantasy Support Team

The following exercise will give you experience in using your intuition as you ask for and receive the support and wisdom of your Fantasy Support Team.

For this exercise, you can use the one scary thing you used with your SST or you can use another scary thing that's a challenge for you.

Complete this sentence: One thing I'm afraid to do is

Relax and get comfortable. Take three deep relaxing breaths, center yourself, and imagine that you have your entire Fantasy Support Team in front of you. Select one of the members and ask for information that will be of benefit to you regarding this challenge. Talk to them freely and ask as many questions as you like, just as if they were truly sitting in front of you.

When you're complete with the information you've received from one of the members, write it down here or have your assistant, friend, or life coach take notes for you. Then move on to the next team member. Continue this process until you're complete with all your conversations.

1.

2.

3.

4.

5.

What is the theme of everyone's information and advice to you on this issue?

What is the most valuable information you received?

You can combine your Fantasy Support Team and your Spiritual Support Team for a double whammy, extra powerful Super Support Team. You can also change, add, or delete members at any time. It's *your* support team. You can do whatever you want with them!

Remember to relax and have fun with this. The more you play with this the easier you'll find information coming to you.

A Letter From Your Future Self

You have the ability to access your future and bring back knowledge and wisdom that will assist you now. This resource will enable you to envision current circumstances and events from the perspective of a future time, giving you unique and highly valuable information that you can use now.

One easy way to access your future and bring back knowledge to the present time is to write a letter to yourself as if you are a much older, wiser, and more experienced person.

During this next exercise, you might imagine yourself to be 80 or 90 years old. In this letter you may give advice, support, and encouragement to yourself, as you exist in present time.

Dear

Love,

A few days after you've completed this letter to yourself, read it again. Periodically review it; as time progresses you'll find new wisdom each time you read it.

Walking Backward Through Time

Another way you can access wisdom from another time is by walking backward through time. It's a bit like the letter exercise, but much more detailed. During this exercise you'll experience different time periods of your future, bringing to the present time the wisdom you've gained throughout all these times.

You may want to have a friend or your life coach act as your scribe during this exercise so that you can focus on receiving the information. If you do it alone, have a notepad and pen handy so that you can write down your thoughts as they occur. You won't want to lose any gems of wisdom that you receive while you're doing this exercise.

You'll need eight sheets of paper large enough for you to stand on. Letter size paper works fine for this purpose. On the first paper write "Now." On the second one write "1 month." Continue in this manner using the following time periods: 3 months, 6 months, 1 year, 2 years, 5 years. These are the future time periods you'll be visiting during this exercise.

Now, place the papers on the floor in a line and in sequence, with "Now" at one end and "5 years" at the opposite end. These papers represent a time line. Step onto the first paper marked "Now" *with your back facing the future*. Take a few moments to settle into the energy of being in "Now" and then begin to describe how you're living your life purpose in the present time.

When you feel complete with your description, step *backward* onto the next paper, *continuing to keep your back to the future.* You should now be standing on the paper with "1 month" written on it. Describe how you're living your life purpose as if you actually are one month in the future.

When you're complete with this, step *backward* onto the next paper, which is the paper with "3 months" written on it. Describe how you see yourself living your life purpose three months in the future. Continue this process until you're at "5 years" and have completed the description for that time period.

Now

1 Month

3 Months

6 Months

1 Year

2 Years

5 Years

Step off the paper and review what has been written. Note any new awarenesses or information that you've acquired from the exercise so far.

Now comes the juicy part. Once again, step onto the "5 years" paper, *this time with your back to the "Now" paper* — the present time. Take a moment or two to ground into the energy of being five years into your future. When you're ready, think about what advice you have for yourself from this perspective of having lived your life purpose for five years. What did you do to get to this point? How did you do it? How does it feel?

When you're complete with the wisdom you have to share from this perspective in time, step backward onto the next paper, which is "2 years." Again share the wisdom and knowledge you have from that perspective in time, and when you're complete, step backward onto the next paper. Continue until you're at the present, then step off the paper.

5 Years

2 Years

1 Year

6 Months

3 Months

1 Month

Now

Review your notes, underlining or highlighting those items that stand out for you. What did you gain from this exercise that you can implement now or in the near future to propel you forward even more into living your life purpose?

Support From Animal Spirits

An animal totem is a powerful member to have on your Spiritual Support Team. The use of animal totems is a time-honored system of borrowing strengths and qualities from animals, especially during challenging times. When you take on an animal as your totem, you adopt their energy along with the characteristics and qualities you'd like to have… or have more of. It's like taking vitamins and supplements for your physical health, except this is supplementing strengths and qualities for your spiritual health.

With so many animals to choose from, how do you decide which one is the animal totem for you? There are many methods, such as choosing animals that:

- you're drawn to
- embody the qualities that you currently want or need in your life
- you admire or enjoy
- hold special meaning for you

213

Choose from animals, insects, birds, reptiles, or fish. The animal can be wild or tame. The qualities and strengths of the animal you choose are more important than its shape or species.

Select an animal for your totem to travel with you along your path of living your life purpose.

The animal totem I choose is:

Now write about this animal *as if you are the animal.* What are your habits, behaviors, and strengths? As the animal, what is important to you?

Creating an Animal Totem

You may want a totem as a physical reminder of the qualities and strengths this animal brings you. The Native Americans used natural materials they found in their environs to create their personal animal totem. In the world of today, you have many options available to you:

- buy a stuffed or toy animal
- purchase a picture of your animal totem
- create a collage, using pictures of your chosen animal
- draw or paint a picture of your animal totem
- make a totem as the Native Americans did using found natural objects

Once you have your totem keep it in a place where you'll see it often, so it can best serve as a reminder of the qualities it embodies.

Messages From Animals

Often you're sent messages from the animal world to guide you as you travel along your path. If you heed these messages, you may find new opportunities presenting themselves and your path becoming smoother and more clear.

Animal messengers can be recognized by several characteristics:

- They attract your attention. Often you may find yourself surprisingly mesmerized by their activity or presence.

- They appear at unusual times or in unusual places, such as a coyote or deer in the downtown area of a city.
- They continually or repeatedly make their appearance known to you.

As an example, when my husband and I moved into a new (to us) house, we discovered that it was infested with ants — carpenter ants, sugar ants, and red-headed ants. One of the characteristics of ants is that they work together for the greater good of the community. This house was a real fixer-upper, and definitely needed many people such as roofers and heating/air conditioning installers working together. Friends came to help with some of the heavier work, too. As the work progressed with help from many in our community, the ants disappeared.

The messages of the animals may be found in the qualities they have or in their behavior. A deer may carry the message of wariness or perhaps the need for gentleness. If the deer is a doe with a fawn, it may carry the message of nurturing. This could mean nurturing yourself, someone else, or your project. If the deer is shoving the fawn away in an attempt to wean it, the message may be that it's time to release something that you've been nursing along.

What animal messenger has appeared to you recently?

What are the qualities of this animal?

How was the animal behaving? What was it doing?

How does this relate to an issue you're currently experiencing in regard to living your life purpose?

Requesting an Animal Messenger

If animal messengers don't seem to be appearing to you and you have an issue about which you'd like them to help you gain more clarity, you can request a messenger. The secret is to be alert for the animal after you've requested it.

Think of a situation in which you would like more information from an animal messenger. Then complete the following statement:

I now request an animal messenger share higher wisdom with me so I may more completely understand the situation regarding

Now, go outside. Go for a walk or just sit. Notice the first animal that appears to you. The first animal you see is the messenger. This may be a wild animal, a bird, an insect, or your pet.

What are the characteristics or qualities of this animal?

What is the behavior of the animal?

What new insights do you have about the issue at hand? About yourself?

How does this relate to your situation?

Which of your life values does this animal represent?

Animal Oracles

Circumstances may be such that you're not able to go outdoors to connect with an animal messenger. The weather may be inclimate or you may live in an area where there is scant chance of seeing any animals.

As an alternative resource there are many decks of cards that use animals for their oracles of wisdom, such as The Medicine Cards, Celtic Animal Cards, and Shapeshifter. Another alternative is the book, *Animal Speak* by Ted Andrews, or one that's similar. The animals in these cards or books can be substituted for the appearance of an actual animal.

Think of a situation in which you would like more information from an animal messenger. Then complete the following statement:

I now request an animal messenger share with me higher wisdom so that I may more completely understand the situation regarding

If you're using a deck of cards spread them face down on a table and select a card that you're drawn to either visually or by sensing energy from it with your hand. The animal on the card you've selected is your animal oracle. If you're using a book, randomly select a page in the book and use the animal on that page for your messenger.

What are the characteristics or qualities of this animal?

What new insights do you have about the issue at hand? About yourself?

How does this relate to your situation?

Which of your life values does this animal represent?

In addition to your Personal Support System, you now have your Spiritual Support Team gathered around you. Call on them often for support — whenever you want assistance with problems, challenges, and issues as you go about the business of living your life purpose.

Notes:

Overcoming Fear

Inevitably there will come a point on your journey of living your life purpose where you'll find yourself stuck, slowed down, or even completely stopped from moving forward with your plans. There are lots of impediments that can stop you from moving toward your goal. Resistance, sabotage (yours and other people's), and energy leaks are just a few items on the extensive list of obstacles that can stop your progress dead in its tracks. During your journey you'll no doubt find several more that can be added to the list.

All of these progress blockers have one thing in common. They're all different faces of the same thing — FEAR.

Fear is tricky, slippery, and a master of disguises. It can be exceedingly difficult to identify what you're feeling as fear. It can appear as one of its more obvious symptoms, such as sweaty palms, heart palpitations, and legs of Jell-O. It can also appear in one of its trickier disguises, such as a sudden desire to organize your desk instead of making phone calls to create new business.

In this chapter you'll have an opportunity to work on identifying how fear shows its many faces to you so when it does materialize, you'll be able to easily identify it. It's much easier to deal with a challenge when you can see it.

In the past, fear has proven to be very important, on a personal level as well as collectively as a species. It's *still* very important or it wouldn't be around today. In the beginning of human evolvement fear was needed for survival. When our Neanderthal ancestors felt fear, they knew instantly that it was time to either run for their lives or to fight whatever was facing them.

Today it serves that same purpose of insuring your survival, although it now appears in more subtle forms than monster-size dinosaurs. In fact, the object of fear in current times is most often invisible. Some of the currently more popular fears are failure, rejection, or abandonment. Not being able to see the object of your fear makes fighting it much more difficult than the simple chore our ancestors had. They simply bopped the object of their fear — a dinosaur — over the head with their club.

In this chapter you'll learn how fear affects you mentally and physically. You'll explore the many faces of fear and learn how many of its disguises appear in your life. You'll also learn how to tame your fears and turn them into allies. By the end of this section, you'll have a comfortable working knowledge of your fears and how to use them to your best advantage.

This is Your Brain on Fear

There is a part of your brain that exists solely for your physical survival. It's called the "reptilian" brain because it's been with us for about 100,000,000 years, since the era of the big reptiles — the dinosaurs. This is the first and only part of the human brain our species had for millions of years. The main purpose of this original part of the brain was to protect the physical body from harm, thus continuing the survival of the human species.

As humans evolved, other parts of the brain were formed, such as the limbic system which deals with emotions, and the cerebral portion which is the logical thinking and reasoning part. The reptilian part of your brain is located at the stem of the brain, securely cushioned and protected from injury. In the event of a major injury to your brain, all the other parts of it may stop functioning, but because this part is so well protected it will probably still be ticking. This is a very clever bit of evolution; you can live without logic and reason, you can live without emotions, but you can't live without your physical body.

The reptilian brain is command control for your survival instinct — the "fight or flight" response. During a state of fear, your physiology changes, and your blood is re-routed to that which you need for survival — muscles, heart, lungs, adrenal glands… and your reptilian brain. *All* conscious brain activity goes to your reptilian brain while the activity in the remainder of your brain, the thinking and feeling parts, shuts down.

When you're in the emotional state of fear, and the reptilian portion of your brain is in control, you have *only* two choices — either fighting the fearsome thing or running from it. Everything you do will be in some form of one of those choices.

If you're thinking, "Hoo hah! We're waaay too advanced for that fight or flight stuff," just remember the last time you were in a very disagreeable situation. Did you want to have a nice cozy, chat with the other person and work with them to create a viable solution to your common problem? Not likely. Probably you wanted either to get away and escape their nastiness *or* tell them off. These are flight and fight reactions.

When you're experiencing fear you have no capability for creative or even rational thought. It's all fight or flight, good or bad, me or you, right or wrong. When you're in this state you simply don't have the physiological ability to think of creative, alternative solutions for a win-win solution. Your mental capacity is limited to only two choices — fight or flight.

How This Stops You

As you're hopping and skipping along your path and are beginning to live your life purpose, you'll come up against many challenges that will induce fear within you, which you'll experience to varying degrees. When this happens, your focus will revert to survival as the reptilian brain moves into action, enabling you to see only two solutions — fighting the fearsome object or running away from it. You'll not be in the mental state for creative solutions or focusing on forward progress, and certainly not for achieving success.

Success? Win-win solutions? How could you *possibly* think of them when you're so busy focusing on fighting your fear or running from it?

Don't fret. There are solutions.

A Choiceful State of Being

Julia Cameron in her world-famous book *The Artist's Way* writes about, and for, blocked creatives. That describes not just the writers and artists for whom she initially intended her book, but all of us at one time or another. As you're moving toward living your life purpose, you're creating your life… and creativity doesn't get much bigger than that.

Being blocked is a fearful state of being.

What keeps you blocked and unable to find creative solutions to your challenges is being in a fearful state. It's like a catch 22; you can't find solutions to your problems because your problems keep you in a state of fear where you can't find solutions to your problems. When you're in this state, you're bouncing back and forth between the only two options available to you when your conscious awareness is in your reptilian brain — the two very limiting choices of either flight or fight.

Luckily for you, our brains evolved and you now have additional portions of your brain which you can utilize. The cerebral cortex is one of these "new" areas. It's where you think logically, visualize, and dream. This part of your brain has the capacity to find new opportunities as you "see" the array of choices and solutions available to you.

Using your cerebral brain puts you in a choiceful state of being.

When you move your awareness out of the reptilian part of your brain and into the cerebral cortex you begin to find choices that are *far* better than the limitation of only fight or flight. You begin to see choices for creative solutions leading to collaboration, win/win solutions, harmonious relationships, and most importantly, peace.

Sounds great, doesn't it? But when your consciousness is in the limitation of the fear-based reptilian brain, how do you move it into the creative cerebral cortex? It's quite simple, actually.

Visualization.

When you visualize, you instantly move your awareness out of the reptilian brain and into the cerebral cortex, activating the creative portion of your brain. *Now* you can begin to see more choices about your situation — choices that are more beneficial for you and for all concerned.

Any form of visualization will work. Here are a few suggestions:

> • Imagine a scale from 1 to 10 and rate the intensity of your fear on this scale. As move your consciousness out of your reptilian brain by visualizing the scale, what choices of action do you now see that will move your fear down a few notches?
> • Close your eyes and envision the situation as if it's happening on a stage and you're the director of this play. As you're watching the players — including yourself as the star, of course — how might you make changes to the plot for an equitable outcome?
> • Draw a diagram or mind map of the situation. Begin with diagramming the issue. As you work with it, your awareness will move into your cerebral brain, where you'll begin to see alternatives and choices. Include these new choices in your diagram or map.
> • Use a visual tool, such as a Tarot card. Select a card at random from the deck and describe what's happening in the picture. What choices do the people on the card have in regard to their situation? How does this relate to your situation?

Living in a choiceful state of being gives you the ability to have a creative array of options available to you at all times, keeping you moving toward living your life purpose.

Working With Fear

Fear isn't always something you want to ignore, remove, or change into something more agreeable. Often, fear can be a most valuable ally. During this part of your journey, you'll be doing some exercises designed to assist you not only in identifying your fear, but working with it. Yes, that's correct, working *with* your fear.

We were provided with fear as one of the most valuable tools in the Human Survival Toolkit. Although fear initially served the purpose of keeping us alive (the reptilian brain's mode of survival), it has evolved and now serves some very important functions, as you'll soon discover.

Putting a Face on Your Fears

The first step in working with fear is to identify it. Since most fears today are based on invisible foes, such as rejection or failure, it can be very tricky to spot how it shows up in your life. Fear has the talent of shape-shifting into an endless variety of forms, such as:

- Procrastination
- Perfectionism
- Laziness
- Self-doubt
- Making other things more important (such as sharpening all the pencils)

- Allowing others to sabotage your work
- Sabotaging your own work
- A sudden urge to watch TV or eat chocolate
- Anger
- Resentment

As you can see, fear doesn't always give you sweaty palms, make you shivery, or weaken your knees. Fear is *anything* that stops you from moving toward your goal of living your life purpose, no matter how trivial that thing may seem. It's vitally important for you to recognize how it shows up in your life so you can deal with it and stop it from stopping you. Unidentified, fear has free rein and can run rampant over your life.

How does fear show its face to you? List as many faces as you can think of. When you're done, use this list as a reference and keep it handy, adding to it as you discover more ways that fear shows up in your life.

The Faces of My Fear

1.
2.
3.
4.
5.

The Faces of Other People's Fears

Now why, you might ask, would you give a whit about other people's fears? The answer is simple: their fears can easily become yours.

As you begin moving toward living your life purpose, everyone you know will be more than happy to share their fears with you about the choices you're making. Their intent may not be to burden you with their fear, but to protect you from having any similar bad experiences like the ones they had when they tried to do something challenging. Nevertheless, there is a very real possibility that you will consciously or unconsciously adopt their fears.

Once you acquire fears from other people, they live within you, ever at the ready to let you know how stupid, inconsiderate, incompetent, selfish, or mean you are to even be *thinking* about doing whatever you have planned. There's one quick and easy way to recognize them: their voice is the second one you hear when you think about living your life purpose. The first one is your true self, your higher self.

This voice has been called many things, some of which I don't care to repeat. Others more socially acceptable are the Gremlin, the Inner Critic, the English Teacher, Mr. Black Hat, and Yeahbut. Whatever you call it, know this: *that voice is not your voice and that fear is not your fear.*

There are some very creative methods for silencing this voice, one of which is the exercise that follows.

Conversation With Fear

In the previous exercise you identified some of the faces of your fear, bringing them from the dark unknown into the bright light of reality. Using that information you can now work with fear and use it to your advantage.

Fear serves a more subtle, yet no less important, duty in your life today beyond just keeping you alive. Fear alerts you to a wide variety of potential dangers beyond the physical, such as fear of humiliation, failure, not being loved, rejection, and abandonment. However, it will often put you on alert to protect you from something that no longer exists, never did exist, or is no longer valid for you.

How will you know whether the fear you're experiencing is valid or not? Simple. Just ask. Have a conversation with your fear and ask it some pointed questions, such as:

- What purpose do you serve?
- What are you protecting me from?
- How can you help me achieve my goals now?
- What is the learning you offer to me?

You may be surprised at the volume of information that wants to come forth during this exercise. Before you begin, prepare for it by having a large tablet of paper or a notebook and plenty of pens or pencils so that you won't have to stop in the midst and look for a pen or more paper. When you have your writing materials together and are ready to start, take a few moments to center yourself and focus on this exercise.

You'll be writing your questions and answers in longhand. The reason for this is that when you print, you lift the pen from the paper often during the creation of a single letter, thus breaking the energy flow. Printing is mostly composed of short, abrupt lines while longhand is mostly connected circles and loops. Writing in longhand, or cursive, allows the information to flow more easily, as your pen gently flows across the paper, only lifting from it or stopping when you reach the end of a word. When you're using longhand to write, the body/mind connection is much smoother than when you're printing, allowing for a smoother energy flow between your creative mind and your writing hand.

If you haven't already done so, select one of the faces of fear that you identified in the previous exercise. Then, with your dominant writing hand, write in longhand, don't print, the question.

After you've written the question, shift your pen or pencil to your non-dominant hand and again write, don't print, the answer.

Don't be overly concerned about the appearance of your handwriting. As long as you can read it enough to get the general gist of the information, the quality of your handwriting is sufficient. When you feel complete with the writing of answers from your fear, re-read what you've written. This is a good time to fix any illegible words.

Use this exercise whenever a new face of fear shows up in your life. Focus on what the fear thinks it's protecting you from and how it can help you to move forward on your path of living your life purpose.

The Fear Continuum

There will be occasions when having a nice little chat with your fear won't be enough. Sometimes you'll need to face your fear and charge smack dab into it. It's during these times when you absolutely *must* dive down to the bottom of your fear before you can begin to work with it.

This exercise, The Fear Continuum, will assist you to continue past the shallow surface of your fear to the deeper layers, getting deeper and deeper until you've hit the base of it and can't go any further. Although this may seem challenging, you may be happily surprised, delighted, and amazed at the results.

My own experience during a mentored coaching call serves as an example of how effective this exercise is. During the call, I was working on being unafraid to ask bold questions of my clients. My mentor coach asked me what would happen to me if I asked a bold question.

"They'd get mad at me." I answered.
"And then what would happen?" she retorted.
"They wouldn't like me."
"And then what?"
"They'd go away."
"And then what would happen?"
"I'd be lonely because no one would want to be around me because they don't like me asking them those kinds of questions."
"And then what would happen?"
"I'd be so lonely I wouldn't want to live anymore. I'd die from lack of love."
"And then what?"
"What do you mean, then what? I'm dead!"
"Yeah. Then what?"
"Well, I guess I'd go to Heaven and be in the presence of God."
"OK, let me get this straight," she said. "If you ask bold questions of your clients the worst thing that can happen to you is that you'll get to go to Heaven and hang out with God?"
Silence. Then laughter.

Yes, I now ask bold questions of my clients — without hesitation.

Now it's your turn. You may want to have a friend or your life coach assist you with this exercise. Select an occasion during which you were stopped from moving forward because of fear. For this exercise, the bigger the fear the better.

Describe your action and what stopped you:

Now, imagine what will happen to you if you continue on despite your fear. As you're working through this exercise, it's very important that you keep going until you've absolutely hit bottom. Continue until you can't go any further and you're at the very last thing that will happen to you. You may even have to go beyond dying, as I did during my mentored call.

What will happen to you if you don't let your fear stop you?

And after that, what will happen to you?

And then what?

What will happen to you after that?

233

And then what will happen to you?

Keep going until you absolutely can't go any further. Then, when you think you've truly found bottom, ask yourself one more time, "And then what?"

Now summarize by completing this sentence:
The very worst thing that will happen to me if I

is

Repeat this exercise anytime you find yourself going around and around the same old circle with the same old fear. Discovering the worst thing that can happen to you if you ignore your fear is the best thing you can do. Fears grow in the dark. Bring your fears to the light so you can examine them closely and diminish their power.

Balancing Fear

You have within you a self-regulating scale that keeps a perfect balance between the amounts of desirable and undesirable emotions that you'll allow yourself to feel.

If you could weigh the emotions you feel, then you might say that you allow yourself to feel ten pounds of fear. This also means that your self-balancing scale will allow you to feel ten pounds of whatever you think is the opposite of fear — love, joy, happiness, courage, etc. Ten pounds exactly of fear. Ten pounds exactly of love. No more. No less.

People who are "more emotional" don't have more emotions. They're just more willing to feel greater amounts of emotion at both ends of the scale.

Although people who allow themselves to feel only small amounts of emotion are said to be emotionally balanced, it is a misconception. *Everyone* is emotionally balanced. Some just have larger balancing scales than others.

Artists and other creatives, who are often stereotyped in our society as being emotionally out of balance, are just as balanced emotionally as those who allow themselves a very miniscule amount of emotional feeling. Their emotional balance scale is *perfectly* balanced. They simply allow themselves to experience more tonnage of emotions on both sides of the neutral balance point. They feel more pain and more joy, more anger and more compassion, more love and more hurt… all in perfect balance to each other.

Living your life purpose meanss you'll be experiencing new levels of emotion, both highs and lows. As you expand your life you'll find yourself becoming more impassioned, which means that you'll be feeling more joy, happiness, and excitement. It also means that you'll be experiencing more on the opposite end of the scale, such as more doubt, anger, and fear.

How much are you allowing yourself to feel? Would you like to move the boundaries of your emotions outward and enjoy a richer spectrum of emotions than you now experience?

If you're up to the challenge, then read on.

Comfort Zones and Sabotage

Whenever you're taken beyond your emotional comfort zone you'll do whatever it takes, use whatever remedies you have available, to bring yourself back into the measure of emotion that's comfortable to you. This action of moving back into the emotional comfort zone is called "self medication" and it can take many forms: alcohol, drugs, coffee, sugar, work, sex, TV, etc.

The most common belief held about self-medication is that it's used to avoid or reduce undesirable feelings, such as pain, fear, and anger. However, *self-medication is also used to avoid feeling too good.*

When you're taken out of your comfort zone on the feel-good side of the balance scales, your subconscious mind knows this means that at some point you'll also be taken out of your comfort zone on the feel-bad side. *This is the self-balancing scale at work.* You don't want to feel bad emotions more intensely than you've become accustomed to, so you self-medicate and self-regulate yourself back into the safety of your emotional comfort zone.

If you've ever found yourself saying, "This is too good to be true" or "I can't believe this," it means that you've just been taken out of your comfort zone on the feeling good side of the scale. As soon as you hear these phrases or ones similar to them, know that your automatic balancing system is preparing to swing you back into the comfort zone of your emotional scale. Soon, you'll probably hear words coming from your mouth similar to, "I knew it was too good to last" as you find yourself now sitting inside your comfort zone on your perfectly balanced emotional scale.

This is the point at which you'll see your weight loss plans fail, your exercise programs fall apart, and your new-found strengths scaring you into retreating back to your emotional comfort zone. Sabotage, whether from your conscious mind, your subconscious mind, or someone else's mind, is a form of self-medication. It allows you to move back into your old familiar emotional comfort zone. Your subconscious mind doesn't want you to feel *too* good because if you do, then it knows that feeling too bad is lurking just around the corner.

Living your life purpose isn't about you being trapped in the self-imposed prison of your comfort zone, watching TV until your brains fall out. It means you'll be expanding into a broader scale of emotions, both good and bad, to *fully* experience your life. When you're living the life you agreed to in your Soul Contract you'll experience the entire range and volume of emotions. The more you feel these emotions, the more you know you're on the track to living your life purpose. Growth doesn't happen in the safety of the comfort zone.

How much more joy, excitement, happiness, _____ (fill in the blank with your choice of emotion) would you like to experience?

What would you need to change in order to be at the new level?

What steps might you take to experience the richness of all your emotions?

What will you be doing differently when you're at the new level?

When you experience your new levels of emotion, good and bad, remember that you'll be out of your comfort zone. If things get to be too much for you and you find yourself wanting to jump back into the safety of your comfort zone, return to the Conversation with Fear and the Fear Continuum exercises. Use these two exercises to explore your new and higher level of fear so you gain the new knowledge and wisdom that it's offering you.

Remember, too, that you can always call on the members of your support systems — Personal, Spiritual, and Fantasy. They're ready and waiting to assist you… all you have to do is ask.

As you continue on your path of living your life purpose, you'll have even more wondrous emotions. Remember, your emotions serve as guideposts on your path. The more intense they are, the more clearly they guide you.

Turning Weaknesses into Strengths

Everyone has something they don't like about themselves and you're no exception. You no doubt have qualities and attributes about yourself that you wish you didn't have or could change. Although you may think of these qualities as weaknesses, all qualities have both an undesirable *and* a desirable side to them. For instance, a desirable quality like leadership can also be viewed in an undesirable light as being too controlling. Flexibility can be seen as being wishy-washy. Tidiness or orderliness can be seen as nit-picky.

All undesirable qualities are actually desirable qualities with the volume turned up too high. When you turn the volume down on an undesirable quality, it becomes a desirable quality. Turn down the volume on wishy-washy and you have flexibility. Reduce the volume on nit-picky and you have tidy. Softening control makes it a leadership quality.

What are some of the qualities about yourself that you view as being your weaknesses or undesirable traits? List at least three. Below each one list at least three qualities that turn it into a strength for you, once you turn the volume down a bit.

1. Weakness
    Strengths
    1.
    2.
    3.
2. Weakness
    Strengths
    1.
    2.
    3.

3. Weakness
    Strengths
    1.
    2.
    3.

How are your life values reflected in these qualities?

Keep this list handy for use when you come to a standstill and fearfully think (mistakenly, of course) you just don't have what it takes to do the work. Then use it to remind yourself of all the wonderful strengths you truly do possess. You might want to make copies of it and post them in places where you'll see your strengths often, such as on the wall of your office and on your refrigerator at home.

The Fear of Not Having Enough

The fear of not having enough is directly related to the fear of not being worthy or deserving. This is the same fear that manifests as poverty consciousness and keeps people in survival mode.

That inner voice you hear chattering away inside of you, saying that you can't have the very things you desire most, is keeping you from having not only those particular desires, but also *all* the wondrous things that you deserve. This voice may be the result of programming from your parents, family, and friends, which means that you're living someone else's program. It may be programming from a past lifetime when you took a vow of poverty that's still in effect. Even though that vow is no longer relevant or necessary, you've somehow forgotten to rescind it and it's still functioning. It may be both of these, and more.

This inner voice varies in volume, tone, and persistence in each person. It may be a tiny, distant voice that occasionally whines, or a looming, booming, constantly nagging voice. More than likely it's somewhere in between. The important point is that it's not *your* voice. You couldn't possibly be that mean to yourself, could you?

Of course not. That's why you're here now, working at releasing all the irrelevant causes of fear in your life that aren't yours, but are nevertheless causing your forward movement to be blocked or stymied.

Rescinding Vows That No Longer Serve You

Releasing past vows that are no longer relevant is a necessary step to clearing old beliefs that block you from allowing yourself to have what you want. The past vow might be an official, ceremonial, or ritualistic vow, such as a vow of poverty taken as part of the requirements for you to become a member of a religious sect. The vow may have been stated very casually, such as when you may have said simply and innocently, "Well! I'm never going to do *that* again." *That* being taking a chance on a financial opportunity, trying something new and daring, beginning a relationship with someone out of your ordinary style, or anything that takes you out of your comfort zone.

To rid yourself of these restrictive vows you can easily craft a rescission of them. Below is a sample rescission that you can use as is, or add to it and make it more powerful for you. When you're done with your rescission, read it out loud. You may want to do something extra, such as light a white candle, burn incense, or anything else that will enhance this process for you.

"I hereby rescind any and all vows that I've taken in the past, whether known or unknown to me, that are inappropriate for me now and are blocking my forward movement fully toward living my life purpose."

Write your own rescission here:

The Take-Away Game

This exercise helps you to clearly identify what your Gremlin, Inner Critic, Mr. Blackhat, or Yeahbut is saying in order to keep you from having what you desire.

Select something big, something that you think is out of reach for you but that you *really* desire. It can be something physical, such as a new boat or car, or something intangible, such as self-confidence or peace of mind. Write it in this space:

Now, complete the following sentences:

I can't have it because _____

I can't have it because _____

I can't have it because _____

I can't have it because _____

I can't have it because _____

I don't deserve it because _____

I don't deserve it because _____

I don't deserve it because _____

I don't deserve it because _____

I don't deserve it because _____

Review what you've written and notice how each of these statements reflects a face of fear. What are the particular faces that showed up?

Which of these fears about what you can't have and don't deserve sound like other people's voices? (This is a trick question. *All* of these fears are from other people. Your true, Divine self knows without a molecule of doubt that you deserve to have whatever you want.) Whose voices are they? Note the name(s) next to the fear they shared with you.

Which of your life values are not being honored by these beliefs?

When you get all these fears about why you can't have what you want out of your head and in front of you in black and white, you can work with theem and take them away one by one, using any of the previous exercises in this chapter, until only the truth is left standing. And the truth is this:

> You *do* deserve to have what you desire.
> You *are* worthy.
> You *can* have it.

Living your life purpose is not about denial and suffering for "the cause". It's about joyously using your natural talents and desires to be of the highest service to others.

Notes:

Plugging Your Energy Leaks

Everything in the Universe is composed of energy, including you. Bones, skin, water, rocks, sunlight — all are different forms of energy. What makes a rock different from water is the vibratory rate of the energy that comprises each of them.

Healthy cells in a human body have a vibratory rate of between 62hz and 78hz. Anything that slows the vibratory rate of your physical body creates an energy leak. When this happens, you'll feel weighted down, tired, or lethargic. If the energy leak continues long enough or is potent enough, your body will become imbalanced energetically, and you'll experience illness. This is why it's important for you to pay attention to your energy levels — how much you have, how much you're giving out, and how much you're receiving.

Any shift in movement, whether from one direction to another or from a dead standstill to forward movement, requires overcoming the force of inertia. As you begin to shift from living other people's lives to living *your* life you'll need all the energy you can garner.

You'll find you have much more energy once you're actually living your life purpose. Until that time, however, it's important that you don't run your energy down to zero even before you get to enjoy the soul-deep satisfaction of your life purpose work.

Things that sap your energy can take many forms. Some are blatantly obvious, such as working hard physically, while some are more subtle, such as things in your environment that are broken and need fixing. Some energy leaks are just downright sneaky, like the burden of clutter.

Your Body: The Living Battery

How's your energy right now? Do you feel charged up and ready to go, or do you feel drained?

Your body runs on electromagnetic energy. Everything in your physical body works because of electrical impulses — sparks of energy that send messages to every cell in your body.

When you're low in energy, those electromagnetic impulses that keep your body and mind functioning become weaker and less powerful, just like a battery with a low level charge sends out weak electrical energy. Instead of powerful, brilliant energy, your energetic impulses become dull and weak. They misfire or don't fire at all. This results in thinking that's foggy, emotions that are jumbled, and physical well-being that's threatened.

You're now on your journey of living your life purpose, and that takes energy. When you're low on energy you have only enough for basic survival. If you want to move forward in your life and accomplish your goals easily and quickly, you need to take care of your living battery and keep it charged up.

How Your Living Battery Becomes Depleted

You use up the stored charge of your living battery in numerous ways and in varied amounts. Here's a list of some energy drains that you may be familiar with:

- Stress — emotional and mental
- Healing from an injury or an illness
- Negative thinking — yours and others around you
- Unhealthy eating and drinking
- Being with people who are unbalanced with their own energy, such as those who are needy, passive-aggressive, manipulative, or Drama Kings and Queens

How many ways do you use your stored energy during the day? Make a list of them. *All* of them. If you think something is too unimportant to note, write it down anyway. If it's an energy drain, it's important. The dome light in your car takes a very small amount of juice to run. However, if it's left on overnight it'll drain all the juice from your car battery. Same goes for the small things in your life. *All* energy drains are important. Begin your list here and continue on another sheet of paper if necessary:

1.
2.
3.
4.
5.
6.
7.
8.
9.
10.

Keep this list handy and when you feel tired or drained, use it to help you discern what's draining the energy from your living battery. Add new items to your list as you identify them and notice if there's a pattern to your energy drains.

Which of your life values are not being honored in these items that drain your energy? Next to the energy-draining item jot down the value that's being disregarded, paying extra attention to those that are repeated.

How Your Living Battery is Recharged

Of course you know that a good night's sleep, eating healthy food, and taking short breaks or nice, long vacations from work will recharge you. There are many more ways to recharge your living battery.

Drinking sufficient water is *very* essential in recharging your battery. Remember that water conducts electricity. If the battery in your car goes dry, you have a dead battery. You can put a battery charger on it all day, but it won't take a charge if there's no water in it. Likewise, if you aren't sufficiently hydrated, your living battery won't be able to accept the recharging you give it.

Not only must you give your living battery sufficient water, but the water must be pure and clean. If you put muddy water in your car battery, you'll ruin it. The same is true with your living battery. Tap water contains chlorine, which kills bacteria — *all* bacteria, including the good ones that you need in order for your body to be healthy and function optimally. Some tap water also contains fluoride, which has been found to damage the thyroid gland. Make sure the water you put in your living battery doesn't do more damage than good. Drink filtered or distilled water.

There are other things you can do during the day to recharge your living battery, such as :

- Listening to uplifting music
- Reading, hearing, or thinking inspirational thoughts
- Viewing things that give you joy
- Laughing
- Connecting with your Higher Self, your angels, your Spirit Guides, etc.
- Napping or meditating
- Breathing from your belly, not your upper chest

What are other things you might do to recharge your living battery so you're operating at maximum power?

1.
2.
3.
4.
5.
6.
7.
8.
9.
10.

Post this list in a place where you can refer to it easily. When you feel your living battery beginning to lose its charge, refer to your list of "recharging stations" and make use of one or more of them.

Conflict

There's nothing like the push-me-pull-me dynamic of conflict to use up all your energy. It doesn't matter whether the conflict is caused by the many outside sources you're exposed to every day or whether the cause is internal, such as a need for you to make a decision. Conflict uses up an extraordinary amount of energy.

In the following exercises, you'll explore some of the ways in which conflict can appear in your life. Sometimes it's obvious, but other times it can sneak up on you when you least expect it and appear in places you'd never suspect. These exercises will alert you to the possibility of conflict so you're better prepared when it does crop up.

Saying Yes/Saying No

Life is full of choices. Creating a life based on living your life purpose means making new choices that may have a profound affect on existing aspects of your life. When you say "yes" to something, you're also saying "no" to something else, and sometimes this creates a conflict of energy.

The Saying Yes/Saying No exercise helps you clarify those potential areas of conflict so that you'll be prepared to deal with them when they come up, lessening the chances of them stopping your forward movement.

Sit quietly for a few moments before you begin, and think about what you'll be doing when you're living your life purpose. When you're ready, complete these phrases with the first things that come to mind.

By saying YES to
I am saying NO to

By saying YES to
I am saying NO to

By saying YES to
I am saying NO to

By saying YES to
I am saying NO to

By saying YES to
I am saying NO to

What conflicts do you see that might cause you to use up energy?

How might you prevent these conflicts?

What other insights did you gain from this exercise?

Which of your life values appeared in this exercise?

More or Less

A first cousin to the Saying Yes/Saying No exercise is the More or Less exercise. It offers a different perspective on how potential conflicts might show up in your life.

List five things that you want more of in your life:

1.

2.

3.

4.

5.

List five things that you want less of in your life:

1.

2.

3.

4.

5.

What relationships do you see between what you want more of and what you want less of?

What are the conflicts between what you want and what you don't want? The trade-offs?

How might these drain your energy and impede your forward movement?

How did your life values show up?

Empowering Language

Words have power beyond their importance as a communication device. Each word you speak has a vibrational signature that triggers certain responses, memories, and thought processes in the people who are receiving their energy. These people include yourself.

The words you use describe your version of reality and are heard not only by others, but more importantly by you. As you speak, your ears are hearing what you say. As you write your words, your eyes are reading them. You, too, are receiving the vibrations and the message of your own words.

Words are not just bits of communication. They're tools with which you're programming your life. The language you habitually use affects not only how you communicate with yourself and others, it affects how *you* experience your life. You create your reality with the words you choose.

Change Your Language > Change Your Life

The language you use can empower you and put you in control of your life. It can also have the opposite effect. It can disempower you, placing you in victim position and at the mercy of other people and *their* wants, desires, and whims. Further, disempowering language makes you a victim of circumstances, events, and your environment.

By consciously changing the disempowering words you've been habitually using into empowering words, you can change your life. Yes, it's that simple.

Listed below are disempowering words and phrases. Next to each are empowering word choices.

Disempowering	Empowering
should	choose, desire, want, could
need to	want to, choose to
have to	desire to
can't	am not willing to
always, never	sometimes, often, seldom
must	choose, desire
but	and
try	intend, aim
nah, nope, huh-uh	No
yeah, uh-huh	Yes
just, only	I AM
maybe	
you make me	I feel, I am
if only	next time
problem	opportunity

Take the Empowering Language Challenge!

Use a disempowering word or phrase, such as "should" or "have to" in a sentence. An example might be, "I should mow the lawn" or "I have to mow the lawn." Say the statement out loud, and take a moment to notice how you feel. Pay attention to whether you feel lighter or heavier, more energetic or less, filled with joy and happiness or with dread and anxiety. Notice the tone and volume of your voice.

Now select an empowering word or phrase and repeat the statement out loud, this time using a word from the empowering language column. Notice how your voice sounded this time as opposed to how it sounded the first time. How do you feel when you use the empowering language as opposed to when you used the disempowering language?

"Shoulding" All Over Yourself

"Should" is probably the most used of all the self-abusive disempowering words. It's so common that most people don't even realize they're using it. Here are a few examples:

- "Well, I should get off the phone now."
- "I should know better."
- "I should call them and thank them."
- "Somebody should do something about this." (*This* is the ultimate victim statement, insinuating that the speaker has no power to do anything about the situation.)

Here's the truth about "should." The voice that you hear telling you what you "should" and "shouldn't" do *is not your voice*. It's somebody else's voice telling you what *they* want you to do.

This person may or may not actually be in front of you. Typically, the voice with the "should" is one that's still hanging around from your childhood. When you were growing up, you were told you "should" do something or "shouldn't" do something else in order to be a good little child.

Your inner child is still trying to be that good little girl or boy by doing what it thinks it "should" be doing. As an adult, you still think that doing what you "should," will make you a good person. It doesn't. It makes you resentful, frustrated, angry, and depressed.

Ironically, rather than motivating you, "shoulding" sets up resistance within you, almost guaranteeing that whatever you "should" do, you won't. "Should" has nothing to do with reality. As soon as you hear a "should," you can expect that whatever follows will most likely not occur.

What are some of the "shoulds" or "shouldn'ts" that you commonly use on yourself?

1.
Whose voice is it?
How would you change this "should"?

2.
Whose voice is it?
How would you change this "should"?

3.
Whose voice is it?
How would you change this "should"?

4.
Whose voice is it?
How would you change this "should"?

5.
Whose voice is it?
How would you change this "should"?

As you're thinking of these "shoulds" and working with them, how are they affecting your energy level?

How have these "shoulding" messages affected your choices?

What are some of the "shoulds" or "shouldn'ts" that are currently being used on you by other people?

1.
2.
3.
4.
5.

What effect do these "shoulds" have on your energy level?

How have they affected your choices about them?

What results have they produced or not produced?

Which of your life values are not being honored in these "shoulds" and "shouldn'ts"?

Power Down Your Negative Emotions

You are *not* a helpless victim of your emotions. You have the power to increase or decrease the negative energy you feel that accompanies emotions such as anger, fear, and depression. Just like the use of empowering language, all it takes to control the intensity of your emotions is changing the words you habitually use to describe what you're feeling. You can choose to diffuse the intensity of your emotions by describing them with words that are less volatile.

The ability to defuse your emotions at will is very useful. There are times when it's simply not appropriate or beneficial to blow your stack or burst into tears. You may be in an important meeting or dealing with a rude customer when you suddenly feel your anger flare. Reducing the intensity of your   ·   "
you to function more efficiently than if you give all control away to your anger.

By decreasing the intensity of your emotions with your choice of language, whether spoken aloud to others or silently to yourself, you can remain calmer and more emotionally stable. Then, when circumstances are more suitable, such as in the privacy of your home, you can luxuriate in a full-blown rant.

Granted, sometimes it's not only desirable, it's undeniably necessary to have a Pity Party or to throw a real tantrum just so you can release some pent up emotions. But if you *habitually* allow yourself to intensify your negative emotions with careless use of language, you're wasting precious energy on something that is *not* productive and will *not* assist you in attaining your goal of living your life purpose.

The point is, you have the power to choose how much of any emotion you wish to feel. You are *not* a powerless victim of your emotions. You can increase or decrease them according to how you choose to describe them, both to yourself and to others.

Below is a chart of some negative emotional expressions as they're commonly used. Next to them are some alternatives that you can use to reduce the intensity of them.

Note: This exercise is not designed to turn negative emotions into positive ones. Nor is it intended to stop your emotions. Its purpose is to allow you to feel the emotion, while controlling the level of intensity so you can still function optimally. When you find that your emotions are inhibiting you from functioning at your best, power down the emotion by choosing the words you use to describe how you're feeling – both to yourself and to others.

Negative Emotion or Expression	Less Intense
I'm angry	I'm peeved
I'm afraid	I'm uncomfortable
I'm depressed	I'm moving up
I'm disgusted	I'm surprised
I'm furious	I'm annoyed
I'm hurt	I'm bothered
I'm exhausted	I'm not very energetic
I'm nervous	I'm energized
I'm overwhelmed	I'm in demand
I'm petrified	I'm challenged
I'm sick	I'm cleansing
I'm stupid	I'm learning
I'm scared	I'm excited

Try a few of these to see how effective they are. State out loud one of the powered up negative statements on the left. Then take a moment as you sense how you feel. Now state aloud the powered down version. Do you sense the lowered intensity of emotional energy in your body?

Shifting your language so that it's less powerful in the negative sense not only lowers *your* negative energy, it also affects the energy and emotions of those around you. Imagine the response you'll get when you state to those around you that you're annoyed or peeved rather than announcing that you're furious or livid with anger. When negative emotions are less intense, you'll find it's much easier for everyone to find workable solutions to the issues at hand.

Notice how you typically describe your negative emotions. If they're not on the list above, add them and then create an alternative that's less intense. Practice saying the alternatives until you're comfortable with them.

Turbo-charge Your Language

As you're learning, words have the power to change your energy. You know that empowering language will take you out of victim stance — an energy sucking position if there ever was one. You also know how to diminish your negative emotions by shifting the words you use to describe how you feel to less intense versions.

Now you'll learn how to use words to *increase* your positive energy and that of others around you, by simply choosing the words to describe how you're feeling.

What is your typical response when someone asks you, "How are you?" What words do you habitually use to answer them? Do you usually say, "oh, fine," in a tone of voice that drops to the ground? If so, each time you answer like that you're bringing your energy — and the energy of others around you — down to the ground along with your tone of voice.

How about raising everyone's energy instead?

On the left of the chart below are some words and phrases that are common responses people use when they meet and ask, "How are you?" To the right are some alternatives that, when used, will raise your energy, the energy of the others around you, *and* the energy of the dynamics between you.

Good	GREAT!
I'm all right	I'm superb
I'm fine	I'm awesome
I'm good	I'm great
I'm great	I'm incredible
I'm enthusiastic	I'm turbo-charged
I'm excited	I'm ecstatic
I'm great	I'm outta this world
I'm cool	I'm outrageous
I'm okay	I'm fantastic
I'm pretty good	I'm fabulous
I'm pumped	I'm soaring
I'm terrific	I'm ecstatic
I'm confident	I'm unstoppable

Experience the difference. State aloud your normal response to the "How are you?" question. Take a moment to sense how your energy feels. Now choose a turbo-charged response and state it out loud. Did you notice a difference in your level of energy after you used the turbo-charged response?

Pick one or two of your favorite turbo-charged responses to "how are you?" Practice saying them until you're comfortable doing it.

For the next week, whenever someone asks you how you are, use the alternate and notice how you feel after you say your new response.

Notice also the difference in how people react to your new turbo-charged response. One client who tested her new powered-up responses found that most people smiled brightly at her and her new, upbeat replies. She was not only lifting her energy, she was raising the energy of all the people with whom she interacted.

The Energy of Clutter

Clutter is one of the biggest energy drains in your life. The weight of even *thinking* about it burdens you and drags your energy down to just above ground height. All you have to do is look at clutter for it to suck your energy. Each time you use your precious brain power to think about how you "should" clean up your desk, your office, your garage, your car, your Rolodex, etc., your energy becomes even more drained.

Everything you own is connected to you energetically. The more stuff you have, the more opportunities you have for those things to drain your energy.

The art and science of Feng Shui is based on the belief that healthy, strong chi, or life force energy, needs to be moving and flowing. When it flows unrestricted along a desirable path, the result is good health, wealth, and happiness. The most common cure for correcting an undesirable energy flow using Feng Shui methods to is remove clutter.

My personal experience demonstrates that it really works. After reading a few books on Feng Shui, I cleared out some of the clutter in my office. I gave an old printer and an old fax machine to a local thrift store. I cleaned out my files and threw away old manuals for computer programs I no longer owned. I patched holes in the walls left by the previous owners, and then painted the room. I took a broken office chair and book case I no longer used to the local thrift store

Just these few Feng Shui fixes changed the energy in my office so that it felt much clearer and lighter. I was able to work more efficiently and, best of all, it cleared the blockage of energy so it could flow more smoothly. It opened up the path for three new clients to connect with me.

Clutter invades all facets of our lives — at home, work, school, and at play. It can invade a room, house, yard, car, garage, and your office. Clutter can also make a mess of your time, with a too-full schedule of "important" things to do.

Clutter is not just the piles and stacks of stuff. It's all those things that don't work for you, or worse, don't work at all, yet are still included in your life, such as:

- a closet full of clothes that don't fit your body or your lifestyle anymore
- broken items that you intend to fix someday
- participation in activities that no longer bring you joy or satisfaction
- people whose company has become a chore to you

Clear the Clutter

Use the following exercise to get a clear picture of where clutter has accumulated in your life and is blocking your energy flow.

List three things in each of the following areas that are cluttering your life and blocking the smooth flow of energy:

Office

1.

2.

3.

Home

1.

2.

3.

Car

1.

2.

3.

Address Book/Rolodex/Palm Pilot

1.

2.

3.

Friends

1.

2.

3.

Computer

1.

2.

3.

Now, decide what you're going to do about each item. Write your intended action next to the item, along with the date by which you'll do it. Imagine the great satisfaction you'll experience as you take care of these items and how your energy will be lifted when you cross them off your list. If you want additional support in clearing these items of clutter from your life, ask a member of your Personal Support Team or your life coach to hold you accountable.

Notice how different the areas feel as you clean up the clutter. How else are you experiencing the change of energy? Are you feeling more energetic? Has more business appeared as a result of cleaning up the clutter? Have your personal relationships changed?

Beyond the Obvious Clutter

Things that don't bring you joy or satisfaction are another form of clutter. Every time you look at them, they lower your energy. These items may have been gifts and you think you "should" keep them for sentimental value or because the person who gave them to you might want to see you with their gift. Sometimes it can be a thing that you bought and because you paid a hefty sum for it, you're resistant to letting it go. Whatever your reason for hanging on to anything that doesn't give you pleasure, you have a better reason for letting go of it. *It's draining your life force.*

The things you absolutely love lift up your spirits and your energy each time you look at them. Surround yourself with only possessions that you enjoy, and the energy of your home and office will be of the highest and clearest energy. It will be a joy for you and others simply to step into your living space, as the clear energy raises the energy of everyone who walks into it.

The Energy of Your Wealth Corner

A very fun Feng Shui cure for bringing more wealth into a space is to buy something that's so beautiful you absolutely love it *and* it costs just a bit more than you're comfortable paying. You may even think you can't afford it or shouldn't buy it because it costs so much. Buy it anyway and place it in the wealth corner of your home or office. It will raise your energy and your sense of self worth every time you look at it.

If you're not familiar with the designations of the corners in Feng Shui, the wealth corner is the far left corner of the room as you're standing in the doorway looking into the room.

In the wealth corner of my office is the certificate I received when I graduated from The Academy for Coach Training. The certificate itself represented an amount of money that I thought I couldn't afford to spend on schooling, but did anyway. I decided that I'd frame the certificate and that the price of the framing would be no object. I went to the best frame shop in town and as I entered the store I saw the perfect frame. I gulped when they told me how much it would be for the framing, and did it anyway. To this day I get great enjoyment from looking at my beautifully framed certificate as it hangs in the wealth corner of my office. Each time I gaze at it, I remember how expensive I thought it was, and I smile as I feel my sense of self worth ratchet up a couple of notches.

Energy Inventory

Take a look at the objects you surround yourself with every day. As you look at each one, stop for a moment and notice your energy level. Does just looking at it increase your energy or does it lower it? Do you get enjoyment from looking at it or from using it, or does it have the opposite effect? List at least five items in your home that no longer bring you joy and, instead, send your energy into a nose dive every time you look at them.

1.

2.

3.

4.

5.

Next to each item write down what you'll do to fix the energy of these items: repair, remodel, restore, or replace them. Note also the date by which you will complete these tasks. Share your list with someone from your Personal Support System or your life coach, and ask to be held accountable for these actions.

Each time you bring another item into your living or work space, notice how your energy changes when you're in these spaces. Notice changes in other people as they, too, experience the changes.

The Total Weight

This fun and unusual exercise will give you a very real experience of how much your inner conflicts, your disempowering language, your clutter and all the other energy leaks are weighing you down.

Go for a walk on a beach and take with you a piece of chalk and a backpack or bag. As you're walking, think of one of your energy leaks that you've identified in this chapter. Select a rock that represents how big this energy leak is in your life and use the chalk to write the name of it on the rock. Put the rock in your bag or backpack and continue on. Repeat this until either you have rocks for all the energy leaks in your life or you've run out of room.

As you continue your walk on the beach, notice how much more energy it takes to carry them with you. Relate their weight and the extra energy you're expending as you carry them to the extra energy that you're spending on the *real* energy leaks.

When you're complete with this part of the exercise, stop and set down the bag or backpack. Open it and spread your energy leaks out so you can take a look at them.

Which of your energy leaks are the biggest and take the most of your energy?

Which are the easiest to let go?

How are each of the energy leaks not honoring your life values?

What other observations do you have about your energy leaks?

Completion

Completion doesn't always mean resolution of an issue or finishing a task. It can mean simply being done emotionally with the experience and releasing it. How do you know when you're complete with something? You become bored with it. You sense that there's nothing more you want to do about it. It no longer holds the attraction or fascination for you that it once did.

Holding on to things, experiences, and people beyond the time when you're complete with them is another form of clutter and will surely drain your energy.

List five things that you suspect you're complete with but are still holding on to.

1.
2.
3.
4.
5.

What do you need to do in order to be absolutely sure that you're complete with each of them? It may be a physical action or it may be emotional or spiritual, such as forgiveness or releasing perfection. Whatever it is, write it down after the corresponding item on your list.

When you're complete with an item, write it on a piece of paper and fold it three times. Release it to God, the Universe, or Spirit for transformation to its highest form by lighting it on fire and burning it. Be sure to do this safely! Notice how your energy rises as you acknowledge your completeness with each item and release it by burning the paper it's written on.

Notes

Self Care

Too much of a good thing is wonderful.
Mae West

You are enough. You have enough. You do enough.
Sark

Treating my self like a precious object will make me strong.
Julia Cameron

These women know the important of taking care of yourself. If you don't take care of your body on a regular basis, you won't have the energy and strength to achieve your goals. It's that simple. Consider this: what fun will it be to live your life purpose if you're exhausted or sick?

Self care involves recognizing when you're getting tired, stressed, or bored, *before* you bottom out. It's imperative that you spot a potential burn-out or stress-caused illness before it happens so you have the energy to continue on your journey of service to others — the service that only you can do by fully living your life purpose.

271

In this section, you'll define the warnings that alert you when you're heading toward being over-worked, over-tired, and over-stressed. You'll explore different ways of taking care of yourself during stressful and exhausting times. You'll also set up a system so that taking care of yourself on a daily basis becomes as natural and normal as brushing your teeth every morning.

A system of caring for yourself is *not* a luxury. Nor is it an option. You're a precious being of great value, and like anything that's of great value, you deserve to have the best of care. You'll retain your value *only* if you're kept in optimum condition. In order for you to do the important work you chose this lifetime, you must be able to function at your optimum.

How can you possibly be of service to others if you're too tired or too sick to do anything but lie in bed?

Any flight in a commercial plane includes pre-flight instructions that the flight attendants give the passengers. In their instructions they tell those who are flying with children that in case of emergency the adult is to put on their oxygen mask first and *then* help the children with their masks. If the adult passes out from lack of oxygen, they aren't going to be able to help the children.

It's the same principal with serving your life purpose. If you're constantly laid up because of stress related illness or pure exhaustion, you're not going to be of much use to those whom you chose to serve this lifetime.

As Buddha said, "*You yourself, as much as anybody in the entire universe, deserve your love and affection.*" Show yourself that you love you by taking good care of the vehicle that carries you on this Earthwalk.

Stress

The root cause of most illnesses is stress in one of its many forms. Although there is a wide array of the forms stress might take, there are two basic types of stress: acute and chronic.

Acute stress is brought on by a traumatic event, which might be physical, such as an accident or injury, or an emotional trauma such as the sudden death of a loved one.

Chronic stress is the continual exposure to undesirable circumstances and/or environments. Some very common causes of chronic stress include being forced to work with people you don't get along with, doing work you detest or that isn't in alignment with your life purpose, and staying in relationships that aren't honoring your life values.

As scientists and doctors are beginning to recognize, stress is the foundation of the majority of many modern day illnesses. Chronic stress is insidious, eating away at your life force and leading to diseases such as cancer, depression, heart disease, fibromyalgia, and Chronic Fatigue Syndrome.

The first step in taking care of yourself is to acquire the awareness of how chronic stress shows up for you.

Symptoms of Stress

Being in a state of stress for a short period of time can sometimes be exhilarating and energizing. Just ask anyone who's working to beat a deadline. But being in a state of continual stress caused by ongoing situations is harmful to your health. It can show up in many ways. For some the symptoms are physical, such as weight gain, weight loss, irregular heartbeat, headaches, and tiredness. For others the symptoms are emotional and include anger, sadness, irritation, depression, annoyance, and sometimes even a lack of emotion. Many experience both physical and emotional symptoms of stress.

Recognizing what you're feeling when you're under stress is of the utmost importance. You can't change or remove the causes of stress unless you can identify them. The first step is identifying how you experience stress in your body.

List as many of your symptoms of stress as you can. Then enlist the aid of those close to you for additional symptoms you may not recognize. It's often much easier for others to see how you react to stress than to see it yourself.

1.
2.
3.
4.
5.
6.
7.
8.
9.
10.
11.
12.
13.
14.
15.

Review this list often to refresh your memory about how stress feels to you. When you feel any of these symptoms, stop what you're doing immediately and make a mental marker of how it feels and what's causing your stress. As you recognize additional ways that stress affects you, add them to your list.

Charting Your Stress

As you go about your busy day, periodicaly take note of how you feel. Rate your stress level from 1 to 10, with one being calm and peacefull and ten on the verge of blowing up.

On your calendar, daytimer, or PDA note your stress rate and the sympton of stress you feel. Also make note of the cause of your stress, if you can identify it.

When you've completed two weeks of this exercise, review the numbers and compare how you've rated the different symptoms of stress. Notice if there are patterns and, if so, make note of them here:

Which of the symptoms had the highest rating?

What was the cause of these high stress ratings? If there are multiple causes, what are the similarities?

Which of your life values were not being honored?

Dealing With Short Term Stress

One of the simplest ways to deal with stress is to live your life so your most important life values are consistently honored with strong personal boundaries. This simple practice will automatically eliminate most of the reasons for chronic stress in your life.

But what about the stress that's short term?

It can still cause you problems, steal your energy, and possibly even affect your health. Take heart. There are things you can do to relieve the stress so that your health — both physical and emotional — isn't affected adversely.

In everyone's life there are unavoidable things, events, and people that are annoying and irritating. The snippy attitude you receive from a sales clerk may not be enough to make you want to spend the time and effort to craft the wording for a personal boundary just for that one incident. But it still causes you stress, and that stress will accumulate in your body unless you do something to release it.

In cases like this, the best thing you can do is to use an antidote. Treat yourself to something you love to do — something that makes you feel good, relaxes and soothes you. You might soak in a hot tub or scented bath, go for a walk in nature, meditate, write, work out, or listen to beautiful music.

List ten of your personal favorites here:

1.
2.
3.
4.
5.
6.
7.
8.
9.
10.

Think of a recent incident that caused you to experience a bit of short-term stress. Which of these remedies might you have utilized to relieve or eliminate your stress?

Keep this list handy and the next time you find yourself gritting your teeth because someone made a stupid mistake that created unnecessary work for you or your computer crashed *again* for the seventeenth time that day, refer to your list and reduce your stress by treating yourself to one of the things on it.

Treating Yourself

The word "treating" in the context of an antidote for stress has a double meaning:
- a reward or special occasion: You might treat yourself or a friend to dinner and a movie.
- method for healing: You might treat a cold by taking extra Vitamin C, resting, and drinking lots of liquids.

When you use one of the remedies you just listed to reduce or eliminate your stress, you're not only giving yourself a treat, you're also giving yourself a healing treatment. You're healing your body from the damages of stress.

Massage is one treat that's more a method for healing than it is a reward, even though many use it as a reward. The touch of another person, when done in an honoring and caring manner, has health benefits that are just now being realized by the traditional medical profession. Scientific research has shown that during a therapeutic massage, blood pressure lowers, adrenaline output reduces, and muscles lose their tenseness.

Aside from all the measurable physical benefits of a massage, there is the immeasurable but immensely more important benefit of human touch. It's been found that babies who don't receive touch from another human are retarded in their physical, emotional, and mental growth. Some believe that without human touch a baby will die.

During times of stress it's even more important for you to treat yourself to a healing massage. At least once a week is recommended. There are many types of massage now: Swedish, sports, Lomi Lomi (Hawaiian), Shiatsu, hot stone (very yummy on a cold, wintry day), lymphatic cleanse, Russian, and Rolfing, to name a few of the more well known forms. Most insurance companies now pay for massages with a licensed massage therapist. If money is an issue, get creative with what you have and offer to trade.

Treat yourself *both* ways with a massage and you'll find you have more energy and greater health, making your path much easier to tread.

Letting Go

These days burnout from stress is becoming as commonplace as Starbucks. It's everywhere! In order to keep up, get ahead, or just stay even, you're working longer and harder. In the majority of households both husband and wife are working full time or more in order to afford a standard of living considered by many to be non-luxurious.

All this working, doing, and being so busy is adding huge amounts of stress to your life. Stress related diseases are on the rise in our country. While you can't go back to the slow, relaxed pace of frontier days, there is a lot you can do to slow down your frantic pace.

Many of the causes of stress in your life don't need to be there in the first place. Examples are:

- Routine chores at home that can be done by someone else, such as cleaning the house, doing the laundry, gardening, and changing the oil in your car
- Intrusions of negative energy, such as news on TV (it's nothing but a list of disasters and is guaranteed to increase your stress level)
- Maxing out your schedule with no space for relaxation and quiet time
- Caffeine and white sugar
- Taking on too many volunteer obligations
- Tasks at work that can be delegated to others

What are some of the stressful things in your life that you can release?

List at least 15 things — large, small, even the seemingly insignificant — that you can release:

1.
2.
3.
4.
5.
6.
7.
8.
9.
10.
11.
12.
13.
14.
15.

How might you release some of them? Next to each one, specify the methods you'll use to release them. Also note by each one the date by which you commit to releasing them.

Review your list and notice which of your life values aren't represented.

For additional support, go back to Chapter 7 and re-read the section on The Art of Delegation (page 170) and the section in Chapter 5 on Urgent and Important (page 89). Then ask one of the members of your Personal Support Team or your life coach to hold you accountable for your commitments to release these stressful items from your life.

Just Say NO!

One of the most simple solutions to relieving stress is often also the most difficult.

Just say "no."

It's not always easy to say, and yet by saying that simple one syllable word at opportune times, you can dramatically reduce the stress in your life.

Imagine if you could say "no" right now to some of the things in your life that are causing you to feel stress in the form of anxiety, resentment, or anger. Imagine for a moment saying "no" without suffering recrimination, guilt or backlash of any kind to those things that are weighing you down and just generally making your life less pleasant. What are these things? Requests from others to volunteer your time? Obligations you've agreed to do but don't really want? Behaviors from others you're tolerating?

Identify at least five of them and list them below:

1.

2.

3.

4.

5.

After you've written them down, imagine yourself actually saying "no" to them. How will you say it? Write the verbiage you'll use in the space after each one.

Now, pick one and actually do it. If possible, do it in person. Simply ask if the person if they have a moment, then deliver your message and thank them for their cooperation. If you can't do it in person, phone the person involved and tell them "no" exactly as you've written it. If you're feeling uncertain about this, go to your Personal Support Team, your Dream Team, or your life coach and get support from them to help you. Remember, that's *their* life purpose!

After you've actually told someone "no," write about your experience in the space below. How did you feel before, during, and after the exercise?

What were the successes you experienced?

Dealing With Major Ongoing Causes of Stress

For minor stressful situations that happen once, only occasionally, or which don't rate highly on your Stress Chart, cures may be as easy and simple as a hot soak in a bath, a walk in nature, or meditation. But sometimes the cause of the stress you're experiencing becomes chronically intense. When this happens, it needs to be dealt with at a deeper and more permanent level so that the situation doesn't begin to deteriorate your emotional and physical health.

The following exercise is based on honoring your life values and will give you the format for digging deep into the root cause of your stress and then exploring different options for curing it.

Describe the situation fully and completely, using additional paper if necessary.

When you're complete with writing about your stressful situation, go back through it and identify *all* of your core life values that are *not* being honored. List them here and describe exactly how they are not being honored. Use additional paper if you need it.

1.

2.

3.

4.

5.

Using your description of how your life values aren't being honored, what are the boundaries that you would like to set so that they *are* honored in this situation? Create at least three boundaries for each value that is not being honored.

Value 1
1.
2.
3.

Value 2
1.
2.
3.

Value 3
1.
2.
3.

Value 4

1.

2.

3.

Value 5

1.

2.

3.

Read each personal boundary aloud, imagining that you're actually speaking it to whoever is involved in the stressful situation. How do you feel after you state each one? Are you completely comfortable or maybe just a little nervous?

Practice saying each of these boundaries until you feel comfortable doing so. Enlist the help of someone from your Personal Support Team or your life coach to role play with you until you're comfortable enough to state them confidently to your boundary violator. Then step into action and do it! Remember, your Personal Support Team exists for the purpose of helping you when you need it.

Routine Self care

Your body is the vehicle that carries you around during this Earthwalk, and like any vehicle, you must take care of it or it will break down. Forget to change the oil in your car and before long you'll need to have a new engine installed or buy another car. You don't have the option of changing your body as easily as you do your car, so it's absolutely vital that you take good care of the body you *do* have. Routine self care makes it easier for your body to serve you well as you live your life purpose.

What do you do for yourself now on a daily basis to take care of your body?

List at least ten things you do now or would like to do every day to keep your body strong and in good health. The self care items can also be a habit you want to eliminate, such as watching news on TV or sugar-laden desserts. Every day for the next week, put a check after each self care item you accomplished for that day.

Self Care Item

1.
2.
3.
4.
5.
6.
7.
8.
9.
10.

Experts say that it takes 28 days to stop an existing habit or to create a new one. Using this list for three more weeks will help you to create new habits so that healthy self care becomes automatic for you.

Take care of your body and it will take care of you.

Rewards

Ahhhh, yes. The best is saved for last, just like the sweetness of dessert after a meal of many nutritious and delicious courses.

Although the information about rewards is at the end of this book, it doesn't mean you should save rewarding yourself until the very end of your journey. Quite the contrary. Rewards are an integral part of your journey. Rewards serve many purposes — as motivators, as markers along the pathway of your journey, and as self care, to name a few.

It's important that you give yourself a reward for each and every step you complete, whether big or small, no matter what the outcome. Rewards serve to encourage you to continue along your path. For each step you take, each effort you make, and each accomplishment you complete, whether you deem it to be a success or a failure (yes, *failure*!) reward yourself.

Rewards as Celebration

You deserve a reward simply for having the initiative and the courage to move into action. The fact that you took a step —

any step, large or small — toward your goal of living your life purpose, rather than succumbing to the force of inertia, is deserving of a reward. Celebrate!

Rewards as Motivators

Using rewards to motivate yourself to do something unpleasant, scary, dreary, or monotonous is a great way to get yourself moving. Sometimes just thinking about the reward waiting for you at the end of a job will be motivation enough to get you to accomplish the work.

As an example, you and I know that it's important to get exercise and stay in shape so that your body has the strength and energy to carry you as you do the sometimes exhausting work of living your life purpose.

For me, staying in shape means a regular exercise program that includes lifting weights. Never has a more boring exercise method been devised unless you consider the monotonous torture of using a treadmill. If death by boredom were a possibility, I'm certain that weight lifting and using a treadmill would be two of the instruments used to that end. In order to motivate myself to lift weights (I sold my treadmill years ago), the reward I give myself at the end of a workout is a soothing soak in my spa. If I really need extra encouragement to get off my behind and work out, I add a beautiful smelling essential oil to the water.

Rewards as Markers

When you reward yourself for an accomplishment, no matter how big or how small, no matter what the outcome of your action, you're setting markers along your path of progress. If you look at your goal of living your life purpose from the perspective of the beginning point, the end can seem light years away. The view from that perception can be daunting and overwhelming, and may be enough to stop many in their tracks.

However, if you mark your progress as you go along you'll be able to see how far you've come… and that's a huge encouragement.

Your journey of living your life purpose is a lifetime event. It's a process that's constantly evolving, growing, and changing with many steps and mini-journeys along the way. If you don't take time to mark the accomplishments it can be difficult for you to recognize that you're actually moving forward and making progress.

A friend, a life coach, or anyone else who is watching you and paying attention to you as you go along your journey, will probably notice the progress you're making. But when you're on the inside looking out, it may seem as if you're standing still, even though you're moving at the speed of light. Using rewards as markers will enable you to see your progress more easily.

This major oversight of not marking all the steps along the way has caused more than one person to give up because they thought they weren't making any progress, when indeed they were. All they needed to do was acknowledge each step they took toward their goal by rewarding themselves, and these markers would have enabled them to see their progress.

Weight loss programs are one example of the successful use of rewards. They usually include regular meetings that the participants are required to attend. A big portion of these meetings is taken up with celebrating any weight loss accomplishments and rewarding the dieters with applause and acknowledgement. If there were no reward and no celebration, these programs would not be nearly as effective.

The same is true of you and your program for living your life purpose. Celebrate your accomplishments with a reward. You'll find that it's easier to recognize the progress you're making on your path if you do.

Rewards as Self Care

Most people believe they have to earn a reward. This belief reeks of the Puritan Work Ethic, guilt brought on by the dreaded "Shoulds" (remember "Shoulds" from Chapter 10 — Energy Leaks?) and thoughts of not being worthy enough to be treated well.

Pay attention here: you deserve to treat yourself to rewards as much as you deserve to take vitamins, exercise, eat well, and perform any other ritual of self care.

Remember, the phrase "treating yourself " can have two different definitions. It can mean giving yourself:

1.   anything that gives you pleasure and enjoyment
2.   medical care

Rewards are both. As you give yourself something that you enjoy, you're giving yourself medical care. You're uplifting your spirits and keeping your energy high. Recent studies show that people who are depressed or despondent have more disease and illnesses than those who are happy and satisfied with their life.

Rewarding yourself is an important part of self care and will help insure that you stay healthy and full of energy so that you can fully live your life purpose.

Timing is Everything

Now that you know all the reasons why rewards are important, when is it a good time for you to reward yourself? It depends on the use of the reward. If you're using it to motivate yourself, the answer is this: immediately after your accomplishment, or as soon as possible.

The next time you have an opportunity to watch anyone training animals, notice that they reward the animal immediately after it does whatever was asked of it. Animal trainers know if they wait until the end of the session, the animal won't understand what the reward is for and may mistake the receipt of the reward for performing an entirely different behavior than the one the trainer wants to encourage. Saving the reward until the end of the training session may also set up undesirable behavior in the animal, causing it to focus on the reward at the end of the session rather than focusing on the work being asked of it during the session. The value of the reward as a training and motivation tool is lost if not used at the appropriate time. A good trainer will reward the animal for performing the desired behavior immediately, so that the animal connects getting a reward with doing what the trainer asks of it.

Your brain works much the same way. You can train it to be more willing to work on a project if you reward yourself as you complete interim goals and immediately at the completion of the entire project. However, if you wait too long after you've accomplished a job to reward yourself, the next time you're facing this same task you won't be so willing to do it. You'll have missed the opportunity to train your brain to look forward to doing the task.

Additionally, waiting to reward yourself until after all your work is done or until the entire project is complete may mean that you never reward yourself. There may be times when you're on a deadline or feel crunched for time and think that you don't have time to stop and enjoy a reward for all your hard work. Wrong! If you don't take the time to reward yourself for your accomplishments along the way, you'll soon end up in burn-out.

What Are Your Rewards?

Rewards don't necessarily have to be big, like taking a trip to Jamaica or spending a week at a spa… although those are mighty nice rewards. The multitude of everyday little things that give you pleasure can be used as rewards. Taking a break from work for a 15 minute power nap, allowing yourself the time to savor a cup of special tea, giving yourself the pleasure of a call to a friend just to chat, meditating for a few minutes — all of these are examples of the small delights that can be used as rewards.

A Million Rewards

Well, you don't really have to list a million rewards right away, but you can begin your million rewards list right now by noting ten small things you can do to reward yourself.

1.

2.

3.

4.

5.

6.

7.

8.

9.

10.

Now list ten medium size rewards you can give yourself. If you can't think of any, look at your list of ten small rewards, and amplify them until they become at least medium sized rewards. For example, if one of your small rewards is a massage, amplify it into a day at the spa or a series of massages.

1.

2.

3.

4.

5.

6.

7.

8.

9.

10.

Of course, you'll want a list of ten HUGE rewards for those times when you've really accomplished a gigantic goal, or when you need some monumental motivation. If you're having difficulty thinking of some massive rewards, review your medium sized rewards and make them bigger. For example, the reward that started out as a massage and grew to a day at the spa could become an entire week at a spa in Palm Springs.

1.

2.

3.

4.

5.

6.

7.

8.

9.

10.

Keep this list handy. Post it where you can see it so whenever you stop for a break, complete a project, or need a motivator, you can easily pick one of your rewards. Feel free to add to this list as often as you think of any new rewards you can give yourself.

Daily Rewards Chart

As you may remember from Chapter 11 — Self Care, it takes 28 days to acquire a new habit. Use this handy list to help you get in the habit of rewarding yourself. Note each day what you did for your reward and what you rewarded yourself for.

Week 1	Reward	Reason
Sunday		
Monday		
Tuesday		
Wednesday		
Thursday		
Friday		
Saturday		

Week 2	Reward	Reason
Sunday		
Monday		
Tuesday		
Wednesday		
Thursday		
Friday		
Saturday		

Week 3	Reward	Reason
Sunday		
Monday		
Tuesday		
Wednesday		
Thursday		
Friday		
Saturday		

Week 4	Reward	Reason
Sunday		
Monday		
Tuesday		
Wednesday		
Thursday		
Friday		
Saturday		

By the time you've completed four weeks of rewarding yourself, your system will be in place and you'll have a new habit of rewarding yourself each time you take a step toward living your life purpose.

The Greatest Reward of All

Of course, the greatest reward you can give yourself — and those you love — is to fully live your life purpose!

FOR EVERYTHING THAT
HAS BEEN...

THANK YOU!!

FOR EVERYTHING THAT
WILL BE...

YES!!

My Support Team

So many people have been supportive in so many ways throughout my journey of living my life purpose and writing this book that it would require another book to list them all. I'm grateful for all of those who, in so many creative ways, honored the contract we crafted before our Earthwalk. I couldn't have asked for better support and guidance.

Especially I'd like to acknowledge
- my husband, Wayne, for his unwavering confidence in me
- my very patient editor Val Dumond (www.valdumond.com)
- Steve Rother and The Group for their perfect and timely messages
- Richard Brownkatz for his enthusiastic way of teaching me how to write way more better
- Kimberly Leonard at bookcovers.com for the great work she and her team did and for being so nice each time I had "just one little tweak" on the book cover design
- Sudie White at Central Plains Publishing for her professionalism and kindness in walking with me through the process of getting a book to print
- Barbara Bingham who was the catalyst for getting me started on An Inner Journey
- Silver Cloud and Jezibel, my two cats who made sure I wasn't lonely even though I was alone while I was writing, re-writing, editing, and re-re-writing

Resources

Life Values:

Awaken the Giant Within (Fireside, 1991), *Unlimited Power* (Fireside, 1997), *Giant Steps* (Fireside, 1994), *Notes From a Friend* (Fireside, 1995) by Anthony Robbins

The Portable Coach by Thomas J. Leonard (Scribner, 1998)

Co-Active Coaching: New Skills for Coaching People Toward Success in Work and Life by Laura Whitworth, Henry Kimsey-House, and Phil Sandahl (Davies-Black Publishing, 1998)

Personal Boundaries:

How to Say No Without Feeling Guilty by Patti Breitman, Connie Hatch (Broadway Books, 2000)

Nonviolent Communication by Marshal B. Rosenberg (Riddle Dancer Press, 2001)

Psychic Protection by Ted Andrews (Dragonhawk, 1998)

Codependent No More by Melody Beattie (Hazelden, 1992)

Adult Children of Abusive Parents by Steven Farmer, M.A., M.F.C.C. (Ballantine Books, 1990)

Manifesting:

Ask and It Is Given: Learning to Manifest Your Desires by Esther and Jerry Hicks (Hay House, 2004)

Creating Money: Keys to Abundance by Sanaya Roman and Duane

Packer (HJ Kramer, Inc., 1988)
Excuse Me, Your Life is Waiting by Lynn Grabhorn (Hampton Roads, 2000)

Law of Attraction by Michael J. Losier (Michael J. Losier, 2003)

Notes From the Universe by Mike Dooley (Totally Unique Thoughts, 2003)

Fear:

The Artist's Way: A Spiritual Path to Higher Creativity by Julia Cameron (Jeremy P. Tarcher/Putnam, 1992)

Failing Forward: Turning Mistakes Into Stepping Stones for Success by John C. Maxwell (Thomas Nelson Publishers, 2000)

Taming Your Gremlin: A Guide to Enjoying Yourself by Richard D. Carson (HarperPerennial 1990)

Energy:

The Feng Shui of Abundance by Suzan Hilton (Broadway Books, 2001)
Sacred Space by Denise Linn (Ballantine Wellspring, 1996)

Planning Tools:

The Mind Map Book by Tony Buzan (Penguin Books, 1993)

Self Care and Rewards:

Eat Mangoes Naked: Finding Pleasure Everywhere and Dancing With the Pits by Sark (Fireside, 2001)

You Can Heal Your Life by Louise Hay (Hay House, 1988)

Your Body Believes Every Word You Say: The Language of the Body/ Mind Connection by Barbara Hoberman Levine (Aslan Publishing, 1991)

Soul Contracts:

Re-member: A Handbook for Human Evolution by Steve Rother and The Group

These are the resources I had at the time this book was printed. For additional resources, visit my website: www.AnInnerJourney.com

Workshops, TeleSeminars, and Intensives

Experience the power of working with a group of people who are embarking on the same journey as you. Join with the energy of others who share the desire to discover their life purpose and begin living it. Get support on your journey in a safe and confidential environment from those who are on the same path and understand what it's like.

Workshops
Designed for groups of up to 20 people, the two and a half day workshops are hands-on and in-depth.

Mini-workshops
The perfect solution for those who want to focus on just one or two portions of An Inner Journey. Great for those who have taken the complete workshop and want to refresh or enhance a portion it. Each mini-workshop is 2 hours.

Teleseminars
Take An Inner Journey in the comfort and convenience of your own home. Teleseminars are an easy and money-wise way to enjoy the workshop.

Private Intensives
Enjoy the personal focus on your life purpose and privacy of your own one-on-one intensive. Includes one evening and two days.

For pricing, schedules, and additional information,
email workshops@AnInnerJourney.com
or visit the website:
www.AnInnerJourney.com

Order Form

Be the "nudge from the Universe" for the people you love. Order extra copies to give as gifts and help the people you care about to live *their* life purpose.

Name _____

Address _____

City _____

State _____ ZIP _____

Phone _____

Email _____

(This is in case we need to contact you about your order.)

Quantity   _____ x $14.95   _____

Shipping   _____

(4.95 plus $1.50 for each additional book)

8.2% sales tax (WA only)   _____

Total   _____

Payment method:

_____ Check or money order enclosed

_____ Visa or Mastercard _ _ _ _ - _ _ _ _ - _ _ _ _ - _ _ _ _

       Exp. Date ___/___

Signature of cardholder _____

Mail: 4514 155th St. NW, Gig Harbor, WA 98332
Phone: 253.853.4033 Fax: 253.853.4034

You can also order online at www.AnInnerJourney.com
For orders to be shipped outside of the US and for quantity
discounts, contact the publisher by email:
orders@AnInnerJourney.com.

Kathy Wilson is a Certified Professional Coach and spiritual teacher whose own inner journey has meandered down many diverse paths. Some of these paths include work as a pea tester, bartender, motel maid, clam digger, logger, construction superintendent, roofing contractor, realtor, landscaper, snowmobile clothing manufacturer, and website designer.

Somewhere along the way she discovered that her life purpose is to assist others to realize *their* life purpose. She draws on the wealth of knowledge and wisdom she's gained throughout her journey, as well as the higher wisdom of her spiritual resources, and shares it with her clients and students as she gently guides them and supports them in finding their own path.

She lives with her husband and two cats in and around the Olympic Peninsula in Washington State.